WHAT, WHY, & HOW?

Bottom-up Answers

Robert Wheeler, PhD

OntosScience Press—St. Louis, Missouri, USA
ISBN: 978-0-578-94516-3
Library of Congress Control Number: 2021913454
Title: *What, Why, & How? Bottom-up Answers*
Author: Robert Wheeler, PhD
Digital distribution | 2021
Paperback | 2021

Printed in the United States

www.ontosscience.com

Contents

Preface

"Let me exhort everyone to do their utmost to think outside and beyond our current circle of ideas. For every idea gained is a hundred years of bondage remitted." (Richard Jefferies, 1883, *The Story of My Heart*)

For most of us, thinking is not something we spend much time thinking about. It takes effort and a lot of energy. Furthermore, we are well occupied with thinking about immediate activities to avoid using that energy for less demanding activities. It is easy for us to stay within our own circle of ideas and avoid going "outside the box." However, most of us at some time reach out for new ideas and answers to deep questions. I remember that first time I was camping out in the back yard, saw the moon at night and had deep thoughts about what else was out there that I could not see. And I still have such deep thoughts despite the knowledge I have now acquired about astronomy and cosmology. Most of us at some time are confronted with questions such as what else is out there, why we are here, where we came from, and where we are going.

The purpose of this book is to facilitate thinking outside and beyond one's current circle of ideas to answer deep questions that I am convinced form the driving force behind the development of our species, culture, and civilization. Like many, I started thinking about these questions at about 13 years of age but pushed them aside because of more pressing immediate concerns. Since then, they emerged occasionally but quickly were submerged again.

My first career was in the military which did not allow much time for pursuing questions non-essential to immediate activities. That is, until the Army sent me to a university for graduate engineering education in preparation for work in aircraft research and development. The sedate academic environment was exhilarating and provided an opportunity for deep questions to once again emerge and be considered. There I was led to psychology that became my second career later after retiring from the military. My expertise then shifted from destruction and killing to contribution and humanitarianism.

This book is my final attempt to share the results of more than 90 years of dynamic experience and learning that came from courage to think outside and beyond the current circle of ideas. These are the things I think are important and if thought about openly by more people would alleviate not only personal problems of individuals but also global problems of societies.

"Whatsoever things are true,
Whatsoever things are honest,
Whatsoever things are just,
Whatsoever things are pure,
Whatsoever things are lovely,
Whatsoever things are of good report;
If there be any virtue,
And if there be any praise,
Think on these things."
(*King James Bible, Philippians IV*)

Introduction

This brief volume is an anthology of independent articles designed originally to stand alone; however, they are arranged in a sequence that supports a theme. That theme is stated at the end of many of the articles to the effect: most personal, domestic, and global problems would be alleviated if our media, politicians, leaders, and educators would emphasize the human need for meaning, purpose, and explanation of existence instead of the current emphasis on consumerism, wealth, power, entertainment, and violence. Since the articles were designed to stand alone explaining a particular aspect of the major theme, some information is repeated. Hopefully, this will not be distracting and will facilitate understanding that article's message. How many times should it be said, "these are important things and if thought about by more people most of the problems of the current world would be greatly reduced."

The first chapter is what inspired this anthology. It started with a request printed in one of the magazines I follow, requesting short articles from readers about the major thing they have learned. Having more than 90 years of learning, I thought that I should have something worthwhile to say. That sets the stage for subsequent chapters that explain and support what I think is important.

The second chapter is an introduction to the basic questions "what am I doing, why am I doing it, and how is it being done?" Is there something more to my life than struggling to meet immediate daily needs? And, what have studies of history, philosophy, and science found out about this as an underlying motivation that energizes our daily struggles to meet immediate needs for existence and for continuation of existence. This "something more" results from an imperative to search for knowledge and explanations that enables improvement in existence. Information about the object of this search which involves the "what and why" is given in Chapter 3.

Chapter 4 is a brief look at history to explain how the need for "something more" has been met in the past, and Chapter 5 explores the involvement of belief and faith. Chapter 6, then, points out the conflict of traditional explanations and dogmatic belief with modern experience and objective knowledge that produces unsettling paradox, dilemma, and uncertainty. Chapter 7 addresses the "how" proposing a solution to this unsettling situation with a philosophy of pragmatic pluralism. Chapter 7 completes a sequence starting with the basic human need, progressing through its ramifications in human life, creation of conflicts, and finally emergence of a possible solution. Subsequent chapters concern important aspects and impacts of the underlying motivation and its relation to everyday needs.

Chapter 8 tackles the perennial problem of how we acquire information and know what is valid, and how we make judgements and draw conclusions. Chapter 9 is about the more recent problem of having an explanation of existence and something to believe in that is compatible with new-found knowledge and experience. Chapter 10 relates happiness, the good life, and life satisfaction with the basic underlying need. Chapter 11 shows the importance of expanding human consciousness to alleviate the conflict between personal freedom and social well-being. The relationship to meaning in life and purpose in life is developed in Chapter 12. Chapter 13 explores the nature of the object sought by the basic need and the three avenues frequently used in its pursuit.

Chapter 14 justifies the use of supernatural considerations to supplement natural information and shows how metaphysics is melding with physics. Chapter 15 asks what happens to our existence when its physical nature is destroyed as predicted by both science and religion, leading to the ultimate long-range question in Chapter 16: can a form of human life be developed, discovered, or emerge that will survive physical destruction so that human existence will continue?

And finally, Chapter 17 attempts to summarize what it all means and why it is important. If you become irritated at the academic textbook sounding information and replicating ideas, jump to Chapter 17 for the "big picture." Then you can go back and get supporting information. The scientific sounding information is needed to reliably support conclusions and show that they are more than just personal ideas.

An epilogue adds hind-sight perspective by looking at the impacts and importance of these out-of-the-box considerations. Since I am close to the end of my personal earthly existence, I could not resist adding an epilogue that puts the concern for human life as we know it on a more personal level. Is it possible for some aspect of personal consciousness to function outside the brain and maybe survive physical death?

Many ideas presented are not original and I have attempted to show their source as well as the source of supporting information for my own ideas. This may not have been completely successful because some of my ideas may have come from years of forgotten sources. A consolidated bibliography is provided to enable further information about citations.

Chapter 1

What I Learned

For more than ninety years, off and on, I have wondered and inquired about my existence; where I came from; why I was here; and where I was going. And this was not just about me—it was about other people too, life in general, and the world. After many years of dynamic experience, productive research, and enlightening study, what have I learned?

I grew up in a comfortable middle-class urban community where most people went to one of the many churches on Sundays; however, religion was not a major concern or an issue of discussion. Most of my friends and acquaintances were just like me, so race and injustice were not an issue either. For me, a major concern was a book I waded through when in junior high school entitled *New Background of science* by James Jeans (1933). Because of that, I was planning to be a scientist. But World War II came on and since military people were so important, I oriented to a military profession. Military duty did not leave time for pursuing deep questions about existence, that was until the Army sent me to a graduate engineering school in preparation for work in aircraft research and development. Being in a civilian environment engulfed in an institution of higher learning and knowledge was exhilarating and liberated me to think about deep questions once again. Now I was able to delve into philosophy but found it too general. Theology was too dogmatic, and psychic studies were too nebulous. Psychology seemed most fruitful, so later after twenty years of military service with eligibility to retire, I went back to school. Once again, I was exhilarated with available knowledge and remained in academia pursuing research, teaching, and work in the fields of health promotion and well-being enhancement. What have I learned?

The most important thing I have learned is that I am not alone in wondering about existence. It seems that all my fellow humans have this wonderment built into them. Whether it evolved through adaption or was implanted by a creator is not as important as recognizing that it is a normal function to look for cause, explanation, and meaning for experiences and activities. These "ultimate concerns" about "whys and wherefores" are not as pressing as meeting immediate needs of daily life, so for many they may be pushed aside out of conscious awareness. Our culture even encourages this by emphasizing "getting and spending." Struggling to meet daily needs and for wealth, power, and success leaves little room for pursuing fuzzy goals for nebulous deep explanations. Those goals are still there, though, and may surface at difficult times, or they may surface as unsettled feelings of dissatisfaction that can lead to confusion, depression, and anxiety. This ultimate concern can be called an "ontological imperative" because it is an unavoidable concern about existence and explanations. (Ontology is the branch of philosophy that studies fundamental being and reality.) It is a desire to reach out to something beyond one's activities of daily life, to something bigger and higher. (explained more in Chapter 2) My research in psychology shows that such concern is a personality trait that exists in everyone but manifest in varying degrees and ways (Wheeler, 2019).

The second most important thing I have learned is that this concern has been a dominant force throughout known human history. It was met either through revelation or through mundane attempts to explain important phenomena and was a basis for religions, cultures, and civilizations. Explanation for some things were readily available, such as "I feel cold because the air temperature has dropped," but why the temperature dropped was more difficult for early people that had yet to develop science. Because natural explanations of ultimate concerns were not available, the ontological imperative frequently invoked or revealed supernatural ones. As these were shared with other people and reinforced, they took on structure and beliefs forming religions that still dominate societies.

Religions became social enterprises that filled many important needs, not only explanation of mysteries, but also physical and mental support, acceptance and positive regard, belongingness and social identity, and salvation and immortality. These benefits required belief and faith in established concepts that became dogma that usually involved a deity or supernatural realm of existence. As knowledge increased and science developed, natural explanations conflicted with dogma causing doubts about many supernatural beliefs. Doubt about faith-based explanations involving deity stimulated scientific explanations and the technological advances that have produced the comforts and capabilities that we now enjoy. However, this has undermined traditional religion and reduced much of religion's benefits for many. A "great paradox" is that both seem to be needed: faith and belief in a religious explanation for ultimate concerns that cannot be provided by science, and science that provides explanation for immediate concerns with material advances while undermining benefits and foundations of religion.

And finally, I have learned that our view is limited, and despite the advances of science, philosophy, and theology, at the present time there is still a vast unknown that may extend to eternity. Recognition of this can be called "nognosticism" which means not knowing and is an alternative to agnosticism which means not knowable. This term also provides an alternative to both theism and atheism. Although anything might be possible, not everything is probable, and we must live in the world as it presents itself to us "here and now" and focus on usefulness and pragmatism, a view of existence that can be called "pragmatic pluralism" (explained more in Chapter 7). Whether our existence was started by a divine creator, or if it emerged only from evolutional adaption is not as important as accepting the need for an explanation as a current state-of-affairs.

Inherent in this state-of-affairs is our need to pursue the ontological imperative and our desire for meaning, purpose, and explanation. Paradox, dilemma, and uncertainty are unavoidable, and they stimulate our vitality and have been a driving force for the advancement of civilization. Can we resolve the great paradox and have it both ways: belief in deity while questioning its nature or validity? Pragmatic pluralism as proposed here answers yes. Plural realities beyond our knowledge may exist, but we must deal practically with the one in which we live. Personal view and concern about something beyond current knowledge can be called "spirituality," and when shared with others can be called "religion" (more on this is in Chapter 4). Spirituality varies among people and religion varies among societies. They vary considerably and they exist in different forms more because they meet different needs rather than being right, wrong, or universal. So, we must be tolerant of other views without sacrificing our own.

We can include in our daily activities tasks that give life meaning, purpose, and explanation if we are conscious of the ontological imperative. How nice it would be if our media, politicians, and educators would publicize this need and emphasize these fundamental issues rather than the current emphasis on consumerism, crime, power, and competition. For individuals it would decrease confusion, anxiety, and depression. For societies it would decrease conflict, aggression, and terrorism.

Chapter 2

Ontological Imperative

Research about human motivation typically involves studies about meeting needs such as job performance, health, comfort, sex, and security. However, studies have recently been extended to underlying factors that energize motives to meet these immediate needs and provide meaning and justification for related efforts. This can be called "basic motivation" or metamotivation (Maslow, 1971). It is the drive to find and have meaningful purpose and explanation for these efforts to meet immediate needs, something more than just maintaining immediate personal existence.

A universal characteristic of normally thinking people is to wonder about why they are here, where they came from, and where they are going—the source, explanation, and meaning of existence. This is the primary or basic motivation that provides fuel for daily activities. History indicates that ever since people have had the capacity to be conscious of self, this underlying motivation has been a major concern and provided foundation for religions and many branches of science. In psychology the fields of existential (May, 1994), humanistic (Severin, 1973), and positive (Seligman, 2011) psychologies have focused on this need through researchers such as William James (1933), Gordon Allport (1955), Viktor Frankl (1997), and Abraham Maslow (1971). More recently Robert Emmons

(1999) has popularized the term "ultimate concerns," and shown its relationship to "personal strivings" and feelings of well-being.

Because the answers to these ultimate concerns are nebulous and difficult to think about, people tend to align themselves with established ideas and beliefs of other people, institutions, or organizations. Such belief systems have formed culture and dominated societies. They range all the way from determinism established by a theistic force to materialism that excludes anything beyond material nature. Psychology research indicates that this wonderment creates an innate need that can be called "ontological imperative" (Wheeler, 2019). Ontos is an ancient Greek word representing being as the fundamental aspect of existence. Ontology is the branch of philosophy that studies the ultimate being and ultimate reality that is the object of the ontological imperative. The use of ontos as the object of the ontological imperative avoids some of the problems associated with use of the terms God and Deity as explained in the next chapter.

Even though the ontological imperative seems to be a universal human characteristic, it is manifest many ways. For many people it is not as pressing as those of daily life such as job, food, and entertainment. The less pressing deep question gets pushed into recesses of the subconscious mind where it either creates an unsettled feeling or surfaces unexpectedly. For many people it is met by subscribing to answers provided by a belief system already established, one learned in childhood or through subsequent experience. In addition to meeting ultimate concerns, these answers provide many other benefits such as belongingness, social support, moral guidance, immortality, and salvation. Even for people who accept those answers, though, an innate desire to learn more about the source and its nature usually lingers.

When a person is consciously concerned with this ontological imperative, two aspects become important. First, what is the imperative? Is it merely about having a goal or a hierarchy of goals? Is it to have a sense of purpose in one's own life, or for the purpose of life in general? Is it about me or about everybody? Much research is available about the role of an individual's sense of meaning and purpose, particularly with their health, well-being, and performance (Hooker, Masters, & Park, 2017). The famous Austrian psychiatrist Viktor Frankl (1997) dealt with this directly and helped set the stage for humanistic and positive psychology by developing a therapy aimed at helping people uncover their "purpose-in-life." What they think it is does not matter, as long as they think that they have one.

The second aspect of the ontological imperative is the nature of its goal, the goal's source, and the nature of that source—what is ultimate reality? Is it a divine force or great architect that designed and created our universe and gave purpose to life, or is it something else that started the evolution of complexity from fundamentals such as forces and fields to particles, then to matter, to life, and finally to humans? Modern science and philosophy have provided support for many theories from theistic design to naturalistic emergence (Wheeler, 2019). Most scientists admit that at the present time, adequate explanation is not objectively known. The nature and source of this ultimate reality is currently beyond the view of science and can only be revealed or speculated. Even the revealed answers of religions are now recognized as interpretations of human minds subject to personal opinions. Objective explanation may even be forever beyond the grasp of human awareness. Whether ultimate reality is God, some other transcendent force, or a mysterious eternity, is not as important as recognizing the importance of its consideration for human well-being.

In the meantime, a major aspect of the imperative is the search for meaning, purpose, and explanation of existence. The study of this is what philosophy calls ontology but a more modern term is "ontosscience" to reflect a bottom-up scientific approach to the ontos as representing the object of ultimate concern. This is basic motivation, energized by the ontological imperative.

Despite our improved standard of living with its comforts and entertainment particularly in the United States, there are increasing rates of depression, anxiety, suicide, and criminality. Many people are dissatisfied and have a feeling of meaninglessness or discontent from wanting something more—something more than their daily struggles and the consumerism, crime, fraud, conflict, and terrorism they are bombarded with by the media. They want something more than politicians and community leaders that push for power and self-interests; something more from educators that cater to radical activists and teach self-enhancement and material wealth; or something more than nations that pursue warfare, global conflict, and violence. All of this is possible if pursuit of the ontological imperative is emphasized and more widely recognized.

How nice it would be if our media, educators, and politicians would emphasize this underlying basic human motivation rather than the motivation for immediate gratifications and thrilling events. Not only would it alleviate personal and domestic problems, it would also reduce global conflicts.

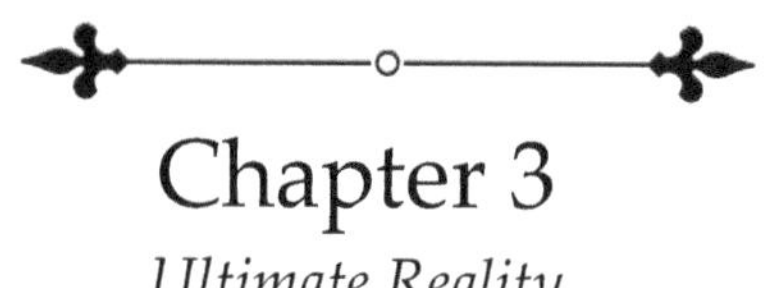

Chapter 3

Ultimate Reality

A major goal of Science, particularly physics, has been development of a global theory that would provide a unified explanation of our observed environment, the elusive Theory of Everything (TOE). Although this effort has been mainly limited to elite individuals in the scientific community, it relates to a fundamental characteristic of all healthy humans. Built into all of us is a need to explain the phenomena we experience in daily life as well as the source, predictability, and meaning of our existence. Concern about a personal TOE (philosophy of life, worldview, etc.) competes with more immediate concerns of daily existence and varies among people, however it has been a dominant social force throughout known human history and is the result of an "ontological imperative" explained in Chapter 2.

In early days, humans did not have formal science to explain the cause of experiences. Why I feel cold was readily seen as nature's drop in the temperature. But, explaining reason for the temperature drop was mysterious, and supernatural explanation was helpful, a process now called "God-of-the-gaps." This accounts for the development of religion and has ameliorated need for a TOE throughout history for many people. It was a reduction of uncertainty that brought people together with shared beliefs and social organizations that developed and perpetuated religions. Dogma helped to relieve some uncertainty but created problems when it conflicted with new information and experience.

Where Western religion explained everything as the work of Deity/God, the advance of science provided more specific natural explanations reducing the need for a Deity/God. The questioning of unyielding dogma brought into question validity of other beliefs and reduced the influence of religion in general. This is unfortunate because in addition to providing a TOE for many people, religious organizations provided social support, moral guidance, object of worship, purpose, forgiveness, immortality, and salvation. Recent surveys show a major drop in traditional religions and belief in God; however, an increase in non-traditional or quasi-religious groups indicates that people still need religion but are unsatisfied with what has been available. The recent increase in domestic crime, murder, and violence has been attributed to decreased influence of organized religion in the United States. It seems that declining influence of an authoritative God has increased lawlessness and lowered sense of meaning in life.

It must be recognized that science has not been able to come up with a TOE mainly because it can only deal with what is observable, while religion which does not have that limitation provides a TOE directly with authority. Unfortunately, the latter is based on revealed or insightful knowledge emerging from humans and are subject to interpretation and questioning. Furthermore, many religious beliefs do not make sense because of conflicts with modern experiences and new objective information, and because of the reluctance of religion to adjust dogma. It is possible that ideas about an omnipotent all-knowing benefactor may have come from human adaption to daily experiences rather than directly from a supernatural deity. We do not really know, but we do know that religions ameliorate many important human needs such as those mentioned in the previous paragraph. It is interesting that many non-theistic organizations also meet many of these needs. But belief in a deity provides some needs such as reliable object of worship, salvation, positive regard, and immortality that are not easily met by non-theistic groups. So, for optimal well-being it seems that we need belief in a deity as well as uncertainty about the belief's validity. This is the "great paradox," belief and doubt about a supernatural deity (further explained in Chapter 6). At the present time, Western religions usually deny or ignore this paradox which adds to discontent. Change is needed and here is an example of possible solution.

A new term free of the encumbrances attached to God, Allah, and Deity might help. A candidate is "ontosreality" which incorporates "ontos," the ancient Greek term representing ultimate being for which nothing proceeded, nothing existed before it; or that existed forever without a beginning. This would be something recognized as beyond our current knowledge that was a forerunner of our existence and gave our existence meaning and purpose. Ontosreality would be like a straw man that could be modified with new knowledge while still providing a deity for different groups of people according to their needs and desires. This is not doing away with God, but it is an attempt to open traditional religions to new information that makes their beliefs and dogma compatible with science findings and modern experiences. It must be recognized that the full nature of ontosreality is not objectively known at the present time, so we must be tolerant of varying needs and interpretations. Could this rejuvenate the declining influence of a moral authority not subject to the vicissitudes of human judgement that is so urgently needed in the United States? And could this globally stimulate the search for its nature and replace competition with cooperation?

Because the nature of ultimate reality is not objectively known at the present time, descriptive terms are used as symbols of nebulous concepts that are easier to grasp. It is not surprising that many of these symbols come to represent dogma that conflict with new scientific findings and current experiences. Which is better: belief in an ultimate reality that can be conceptualized with certainty and fills needs but conflicts with objective knowledge, or belief in an ultimate reality that is currently evolving and compatible with current experiences and knowledge but fraught with uncertainty and fluctuating judgments in human thinking? There are trade-offs worthy of consideration. Ultimate reality is the object of the ontological imperative and human destiny seems to be a search for its nature. Would not our world be better if our media, leaders, educators, and politicians emphasized pursuit of this topic in addition to the current emphasis on wealth, power, conflict, and consumerism?

Chapter 4

Spirituality and Religion

Most people have looked up in the sky on a clear night and wondered about the stars, the vast empty space, and what might lie beyond. Is there an unknown reality beyond what is seen, something that might account for ultimate reality, variously described as God, Truth, Creator, Deity, Light, and Word? The farther astronomers can look out in space, the more they see; and also, the farther physicists can look into the atom, the more they see. The limits of outer space, the "macrocosm," studied by astronomers, and the limits of inner space, the "microcosm," studied by subatomic physicists expand with the increase in observational capabilities. This indicates that both outer and inner space extend beyond what is observable and may even be infinite or eternal (Ellis, 2011). A logical conclusion is that there is more than what is now known, maybe even realities beyond our comprehension. And this observation is made many times by people from their own experiences even when not aware of the sophisticated scientific findings and theorizing.

Research about attribution theory (Heider, 1944) supports a natural propensity for people to attribute cause to the things observed. What is the cause of the hardships and discomforts we struggle with on a daily basis? This extends to deep concerns such as the cause of existence, why am I here? In attempting to provide answers to these deep questions, religions, philosophies, and cultural traditions have developed various beliefs. A common thread in these beliefs is a goal of transcending our current state of existence and accommodating some form of divine ultimate cause. This is captured in Aldous Huxley's (1944) "perennial philosophy," a universal provision in most cultures.

That there must be something beyond our personal physical "life-space" was popularized by psychotherapist Carl Rogers (1961) who showed the benefit of thinking outside of one's own life-space . Whether there is or is not a divine reality beyond our physical senses, people seem to have a need for such a belief, or at least a provision for such a possibility. Psychiatrist Robert Cloninger (2004) effectively supported "self-transcendence" as a personality characteristic that is a desire of people to reach out beyond themselves and experience a unity with a mystical realm. Behavioral geneticist Dean Hamer (2004) has located activity in the brain indicating that even though existence may be a dominant concern, a desire to experience and understand esoteric self-transcendence is genetically based and inherent in our cognitive process. Neurobiologist Kevin Nelson (2011) and radiologist Andrew Newberg (2001) have independently drawn similar conclusions about physiological brain activity associated with these experiences. Dr. Newberg (2010) has taken a brain-based concern with a mystical transcendent realm further supporting neurotheology, a neurological study of religious phenomena.

Science cannot do much about this mysterious realm because it is limited to observation of natural phenomena that is reliable, objectively supported, and independent of opinion or speculation. Religion on the other hand, does not have those constraints and provides explanation for these ultimate concerns by invoking supernatural powers. Religion dominates most cultures but has recently been brought into question by science. Biochemist Stuart Kauffman in his bestselling book *Reinventing the Sacred* (2008) showed how a naturally occurring process of self-organization leads to a human complexity that gives rise to a sense of mysticism and sacredness without need for a supernatural force or a transcendent realm. Also, research about quantum theory has opened the door for non-material cause of our material environment. Abrahamic religions (Judaism, Christianity, Islam) are not yet ready to entertain these issues, although many other religious movements such as Ethical Society, Universal Unitarian Church, Theosophy, and Religious Naturalism recognize a sacredness arising from awe and mystery in nature without the constraints of religious dogma (Goodenough, 1998). These movements are growing in popularity because of the many people who now report themselves as being spiritual but not religious.

All these considerations are summarized in the term spirituality that is increasing in stature mainly because of growing dissatisfaction with traditional religion. Both religious dogma and its opposite, militant atheism, are being questioned. Spirituality is not constrained by either and allows other approaches to ultimate cause. Much is now being published about spirituality; however, most is of esoteric or inspirational nature. The classic textbook *Psychology of Religion* by Spilka, Hood, Hunsberger, and Gorsuch (2003) devotes a few paragraphs in the first two chapters about spirituality being an aspect of religion, and in a later chapter about its role in mysticism; but little about it as a basic psychological characteristic in itself. More detailed information about the relationship of spirituality to religion has been presented in *The Handbook of the Psychology of Religion and Spirituality* (Paloutzian & Park, 2005) and *Psychology, Religion, and Spirituality* (Nelson, 2009), and the reader is referred to those compendiums for additional details and support. Although the information presented here is brief and selective, it is representative of reputable information and does not conflict with the more comprehensive reports of research results.

Spirituality has been defined and measured in many ways. One widely used measure focuses on seeking of meaning, purpose, and transcendence (Ellison, 1983). Other measures were developed using standard statistical psychometric techniques focusing on characteristics independent of other personality factors and related to common aspects of leading spiritual traditions. Studies using these measures have supported spirituality as being an independent personality factor related to other established personality factors and spiritual activities (Rican & Janosova, 2010).

More directly, though, spirituality can be defined as an attitude of concern about an unknown realm that transcends our personal selves. As a personality characteristic, spirituality has been empirically related to mental and physical health and sense of well-being by several researchers (Wheeler, 2019). Some people are more conscious of this concern than others are; some accept a religious belief about it on faith; some set it completely aside; but throughout history, it has been a major force. "Spiritual intelligence" is ability to recognize this basic need and to effectively deal with it (Emmons, 1999). Attempts to obtain replicable information about the validity of spiritual phenomena are ongoing efforts that could be called "ontological research," with "ontological engineering" being attempts to apply this information for the benefit of individuals and society. These are aspects of spirituality that combine science and religion and have the potential to provide beneficial relations between societies vying for power and dominance.

Despite tremendous capabilities of human intelligence, they are limited, and there is a tendency for individuals to latch on to the products of their personal experience and fixate on them as reference points. However, questions about ultimate issues continue, and they have been extensively studied in many different fields. What is the purpose of life? The major conclusion from science (that can be objectively supported) is that the goal of human existence is to exist and to further existence by developing what seems most useful. Ramifications of this are limited only by the extent to which they are considered. Some of the goals that have been objectively supported include self-enhancement, emergence, complexity development, actualization of potential, and flourishing, none of which require a transcendent deity; however, fulfillment has been so difficult that most cultures have historically supported subjective conclusions from religion and philosophy about ultimate goals that could be interpreted as doing God's will, growing closer to a deity, pursuing ultimate creative force, or divine unfolding.

Most concepts of ultimate goals for human life are based on religious beliefs. But philosopher Owen Flanagan (2009) has made a commendable attempt to show that supernaturalism is not necessary with his concept of eudaimonistic flourishing. From his work with neuroscience, he concludes that meaning, spirituality, and transcendence are part of nature, and are best met by flourishing; that is, by living the "good life," experiencing beauty and awe, accepting ultimate explanations as possible myths, and gauging morality on mutual benefits (explored more in Chapter 10).

Gordon Allport's (1955) concept of "religious sentiment" captures this as a cultural tendency, that has been expanded to include "quest" which emphasizes the search for a framework of belief that provides for an ultimate reality (Batson, 1993). Most research about religious belief focuses on the content or end-product of belief as opposed to the search or seeking process. Seeking requires openness to new information and ideas while maintaining sufficient focus and faith to prevent unproductive confusion and vacillation. It is increasingly being recognized that spirituality is basically an ongoing striving process.

A notable attempt to restore spirituality as an essential human striving for ultimate cause or ultimate reality was the publication of *Spiritual Evolution* by the Harvard medical researcher and psychiatrist George Vaillant (2008). He has spent a career studying human development and health, and points out how spirituality evolves as a stimulating process for positive emotions through three avenues: biologically over millions of years of brain development, culturally over thousands of years of social development, and individually over a person's lifetime of personal adjustment. People are hardwired to generate positive emotions that are associated with their essential spiritual beings supporting spirituality as being hardwired in the brain (Heid, 2021). The terms "ultimate concerns" and "ultimate reality" (Emmons, 1999) have become popular, but the term "spirituality" has traditionally captured this concern, and terms such as God, Truth, Creator, Deity, Light, and Word have captured the object of this concern. Spirituality has become a force to open religious dogma to new information about this object of concern.

There are many examples of current movements to open religions to ideas more compatible with scientific findings and modern experiences. One example is the recently popular book *A God That Could Be Real* by Nancy Adams (2015) who is the wife and colleague of astrophysicist Joel Primack. She summarized research about emergence, which she defined as the creation of something new and more than the sum of its parts when complexity has increased enough. She shows how spirituality emerged from the human mind as the brain complexity increased, and that the concept of God emerged from a species-wide collective development of spirituality. It seems that just as the mind emerged from the increased complexity of the brain, spirituality emerged as complexity of the mind increased, and that the deity/deities that dominated histories emerged from the increased complexity of spirituality.

Another example of a reputable system proposed to overcome dissatisfaction with the major traditional religions is panentheism that grew out of process theology. This has been explained by Philip Clayton and Stephen Knapp (2011) by viewing God is an ultimate cause, that people are a part of God, and both are continuing to develop. Theistically oriented people that dislike questionable supernatural claims of religions are being attracted to such a belief system because it is more accommodating of research findings and more consistent with personal experiences.

Some Christian apologists are developing ways to make religious dogma more compatible with experience and science. A good example of this is the work of the noted theologian Gordon Kaufman (2006) that calls for thinking of God not as the creator, but as the creativity that made possible the emergence and development of humans. This Creativity is not an explanation of the ultimate mystery of existence but is a descriptive term for the process. In his book, *Jesus and Creativity*, he summarizes shortcomings in the dualistic picture of Jesus (material and divine) and emphasizes Jesus's teachings that were so radical at the time of Jesus. At the present time a new culture is needed based on Jesus's teachings to subdue instincts of self-preservation and self-defense with a spirit of self-sacrifice for the well-being of humanity. This does not negate Jesus's divinity, but makes it a part of the ultimate mystery of creativity.

Even though use of the term spirituality seems new, its ubiquitous nature can be traced to ancient history. An example of the need to break away from religious constraints and reach for something more is the ancient movement of Freemasonry that traces its history to King Solomon three thousand years ago. It developed as a major organization after the Enlightenment when many people were attempting to shake the shackles of ecclesiastical dogma and political dominance that were creating hardships and subduing a sense of freedom and pursuit of advancement. It continues as a major fraternal organization. Its only dogma is that there is a master Great Architect of the universe who exemplifies Truth. Truth is symbolized as the "Master's Word" and a major goal is attainment of knowledge about the Master's Word and what it stands for. "In the beginning was the Word and the Word was God" (Bible, John 1:1). Freemasonry uses truth in two different ways. One as a tenet advocating honesty and correctness, and the other as ultimate reality symbolized by the Master's Word which has been lost and is the object of search. Because of the allusive nature of the ultimate reality of Truth, allegories and symbols with rituals and ceremonies are used that provide structure for abstract ideas making the pursuit enjoyable and meaningful. There are many interpretations about the meanings of the symbols and rituals providing a varied and tolerant approach to divinity. Even though these interpretations are varied because of an oral tradition, an authoritative summary was assembled by Albert Mackey (1921) in *An Encyclopedia of Freemasonry* that is still in use. The attraction of Freemasonry through the years is an example of the universality of spirituality and the attractions of associated activities such as comradery, fraternity, pageantry, and charity.

Although spirituality is proposed here as a universal human characteristic, it is manifest in many different ways resulting in many forms of commitment. In addition to the impact of varied experiential and social factors, genetic and biological mechanisms have been found to affect the spiritual activity of individuals. A more important affect is the ability to think abstractly allowing people to be concerned about what is beyond immediate experience, but many times the pressures of immediate daily existence over-ride use of that ability. Psychologist Rollo May (1967) described this conflict as the "human dilemma" which is a major source of anxiety that can be treated with existential therapy. Since existence comes first, many people become bogged down in their own personal immediate needs, fears, desires, and pleasures to such an extent that they suppress their sophisticated mental abilities and avoid thinking about these abstract topics. As psychiatrist Erich Fromm (1947) explained in his concept of "existential dichotomy," we tend to subjugate our higher human creative abilities and needs in order to meet our animal needs resulting in an "existential dilemma," conflict between physical and intellectual needs. For Dr. Fromm, this is a major source of anxiety and other mental health problems, so recognizing "higher" needs is essential for good mental health.

It may be helpful to look at a structure of spirituality using dimensions. Abraham Maslow (1968) proposed a widely used motivational structure based on a hierarchy of needs that ranged from "deficiency needs"—physical sustenance, security, social relations, and self-esteem—to actualizing "metaneeds" such as beauty, order, justice, and meaning. Any of these needs may exert a force on the individual; however, thought and action are frequently dominated by the deficiency needs because of the requirements of daily living. Filling metaneeds is secondary activity and their neglect is frequently experienced as insatiable yearning for nebulous satisfaction.

Meeting the deficiency needs can be considered a first dimension of spirituality where concerns of ultimate meaning or transcendence are dormant. When deficiency needs are met sufficiently that a person can devote more thought and activity to other needs, focus can be made on a second dimension involving metaneeds. A third dimension involves making one's belief about this system of needs sensible and compatible with experience and knowledge. Activity involves recognizing shortcomings in established belief systems and the conflicts between them and experience or knowledge. Attempts are made to define concepts in concrete ways so that they can be tested, adjusted, and used for the benefit of oneself and others.

The fourth dimension involves recognition that our cognitive ability, understanding, and knowledge are limited and that there is a vast unknown that extends beyond the observable physical environment and may contain a deity that is some form of nature not yet discovered by science or a deity in a transcendent supernatural realm. Even the famous theoretical physicist Albert Einstein recognized a superior intelligence or spirit that can reveal itself in the knowable world or be a pantheistic force in an unknown world (Calaprice, 2005). Activity in this dimension involves a need to accept these possibilities, to pursue knowledge about them, to contribute to that knowledge, and to help society benefit thereby. Pursuit requires not only dedicated spirituality but also creativity, charisma, and a variety of abilities.

Dimensions 2, 3, and 4 involve activities that Maslow referred to as actualizing. He also provided for a difference between nontranscendent and transcendent actualizers in writings published in 1971. The difference is that where nontranscendent actualizers are focused on achieving personal potentials, transcendent actualizers are focused on factors beyond the self, to something bigger and higher that could be called ultimate reality. Despite our society's dominance with the dimension 1, the others exert a force that may be out of conscious awareness, stored in the unconscious mind. The large percentage of the US population that support established religions are focusing on dimensions 1 and 2 because they are usually meeting metaneeds by using an established belief system and accept that system's application and meaning. Thus, they recognize a higher-level metaneed and are attempting to fill it and help others. The conceptualization, development, and pursuit of transcendent needs dominate dimension 4 activities and involve major factors of spirituality. For people focusing on dimension 4, the underlying ideas (ideation) over-ride worship and faith, and the mechanisms of religious practice become flexible and even superficial. It seems that people investing to some degree in all dimensions have greatest well-being, but the investment of activity and process seems to be much more important than success or the end-product.

This structure of spirituality is consistent with results of extensive research by Lawrence Kohlberg (1984) about moral development and James Fowler (1995) about religious faith development, except that their structures are based on sequential stages rather than dimensions. The term "dimension" is used here to avoid a qualitative judgment about levels or stages of development because dimensions coexist as opposed to being sequential (Anna Freud, 1965). This is illustrated by newborn infants that reach out to explore and learn even when physical needs are met and before they become aware of rewards and punishments (Buhler, 1967).

There are many theories about levels and dimensions of moral and spiritual development culminating with an ultimate stage, but it must be emphasized that these ultimate levels can exist in everyone and may even be prepotent to such an extent that physical needs or other prior sequential stages are over-ridden. Spirituality may lie dormant in one person and be a dominating activity in another person, but it is inherent in all either consciously or subconsciously and is an unavoidable force behind development of religious types of belief systems. All dimensions exist in everyone, but the degree to which they are manifested is quite varied. (Chapter 16 provides more information about this aspect of development.)

Spirituality can be summarized as an attitude of concern about something bigger, better, and transcendent to our daily activities to meet immediate needs. This "something" is more than us personally and can be associated with ultimate reality. Whatever it is, we are doomed to search for it. Being aware of this concern is a first step in feeling that life has meaning and purpose. The second step is activity for the pursuit of the concern. And the third step is experiencing satisfaction from a sense of personal development and contribution to humanity.

When a person's spiritual ideas become sufficiently organized to ameliorate ultimate concerns and augment a worldview, they are usually adopted as a personal belief. When they are shared with other people, they become religion. When they are socially organized, they become institutional religion with procedures, rules, leaders, and dogma. Hopefully, the resulting religion does not deviate from one's personal spiritual ideas enough to make the institutionalized religion unsatisfying. Spirituality can be a lonely thing if not shared with other people.

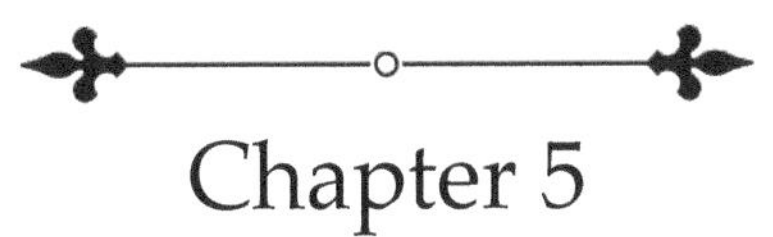

Chapter 5

The Role of Belief

We all have beliefs, and we all have faith. Both involve assumptions that certain things will happen in certain situations with sufficient consistency that we can manage our lives with an acceptable degree of predictability and certainty. Beliefs facilitate our ability to make decisions and take actions without cumbersome thought processes or analyses considering relevant factors, a basis for decision that is immediately available. The term belief is used in many different ways, but the accepted definition includes a state of mind or habit of mind in which trust or confidence is placed in some person or thing, a conviction of the truth. They include short-range things like I believe it is going to rain tomorrow because Channel 5 News said so and I trust them, to long-range things like I believe that God overseas life because I learned that as a kid. Without beliefs, our daily activities would be a chaotic struggle to meet immediate needs. The short-range and long-range beliefs become incorporated into a worldview or philosophy of life that provides predictability, value, purpose, and meaning for daily activities.

Many things interplay to form beliefs. First are genetic characteristics called temperament in psychology. For some, why I am here is not as important as should I take an umbrella today. Such people are by nature more concerned with immediate needs than with whys and wherefores, and they would score lower on personality scales measuring openness and introversion. Others that would score higher on those measures would tend to be concerned with why the rainstorm is predicted and what is its impact. Temperaments are relatively enduring, but the greatest influence on one's set of beliefs is social culture. When we come into this world as an infant our temperaments are pretty well formed, however our memory is empty and strives for input. Early childhood experiences (learning) have a big impact, so our early environment readily forms our first beliefs. Being so dependent at that time on caregivers, makes their beliefs very impressionable. Then as we interact with other people, we are exposed to other beliefs particularly those common in the community, its culture. Despite differences in individuals, the local environment reflects the social culture that adds an important influence independent from early teachings. If one grows up in a Muslim home with belief that five prayers are required each day but lives in a Christian community, soon it is learned that maybe those five prayers are not required. Throughout known history, societies have been dominated by cultural beliefs that usually were based on religious worldview (Gervais, W.; Najle, M.; Caluori, N.; 2021)

Psychology, history, and anthropology indicate that humans have always had a need for explanations of their existence and experiences. They search for and find patterns and consistencies enabling predictions that make their lives manageable and store them away in recesses of memory as beliefs. They are usually based on experience and reliable sources of objective knowledge. But for fundamental questions like, "why am I here?," objective knowledge is not available so assumption, revelation, speculation, creativity, and imagination fill in. Culture moves beyond reliable concrete knowledge into the realm of meta-physical knowledge. Because of the nebulous nature of this realm, reliance is placed on more knowledgeable trusted people who have special insight and can supply esoteric revelations. The results are religious beliefs that are incorporated into local culture and become an important influence on one's own personal beliefs.

Because of modern communications and media accessibility, it is difficult to be unaware of the large number of different societies, each with different culture and religion. Even with the amazing sophistication in civilization resulting from shared cultures, religious based cultural beliefs have provided a vehicle and justification for competition and armed conflict. Sunnis and Shiites are fighting in Iraq, Muslims and Hindus fight in India, Christians and Pagans fight in Nigeria, Jews and Palestinians fight in Gaza, Anglicans and Protestants fight in Ireland, etc. Why do people become so aggressive about their own society's cultural worldview that it is used to justify violence against outsiders? Even if their ideology is the true one, does the suffering caused by violence justify such proselyting attempts? Since individual beliefs are heavily influenced by culture, knowledge of conflicts in cultural beliefs stimulates conflicts in personal beliefs.

Another conflict that causes a state of confusion about religious beliefs is the religion-science issue. Religions have filled many human needs such as social support, belonging, unconditional acceptance, meaning and purpose, social support, immortality, and salvation, but most important is an explanation of the unknown. Belief in a divine power such as God for explanations established religious dogma that have become questionable as conflicting knowledge about natural forces have become available. For example, thunder and lightning at one time were thought to be caused by a wrathful God showing displeasure. Science shows now that thunder and lightning are caused by natural weather factors. That does not rule out God who could still be a determining force, but it does eliminate the need for God to explain thunder and lightning. Although science cannot prove or disprove the existence of God, it has shown that many beliefs based on faith in religious teachings conflict with scientific findings.

The questioning of religious dogma has shaken the foundation of many churches in the United States and is a major reason for their decline in membership and lose of benefits and moral authority for many people. The decrease in religious beliefs is now recognized as a major cause for increase in lawlessness, crime, and violence in the United States as well as for mental health problems such as depression, anxiety, and suicide (PewForum, 2019). Increase in non-traditional churches and non-theistic organizations indicate that people still have a need for traditional benefits of religion but are unsatisfied with what is currently available.

Personal beliefs and cultural beliefs are highly interdependent, and their roles affect all phases of human life from reason to carry the umbrella to reason for existence. Because of the inevitable difference in the personal beliefs of individuals and the cultural beliefs of societies, there may always be conflict. This situation needs to be recognized as a naturally occurring issue that could be complimentary rather than conflicting and could inspire cooperation instead of damaging competition. How nice it would be if media, educators, politicians, and leaders emphasized this as a natural state-of-affairs and encouraged tolerance for the differences and cooperation in belief development. Mental and behavior problems would decrease for individuals, and for societies violence and competition would decrease.

Chapter 6

Great Paradox

Ever since the sixteenth century when Copernicus proposed that church dogma was wrong about the earth being the center of the universe, conflict between religion and science has been an issue. At that time religion and science were in the same field but they soon split apart. Psychology as a study of human nature emerged on the side of science, but recent developments in the objective study of human nature have opened psychology to the religion side as well (Baumeister, 2002; Teo, 2009; Sedikides, 2010).

The secular humanism and militant atheism movements propelled by Paul Kurtz (2007), Richard Dawkins (2006), and others have been effective in showing inconsistencies and illogicalness of beliefs in many traditional religions, but still polls show that most people adhere to organized religious beliefs and believe in some form of a transcendent realm (PewForum, 2019). The continued popularity of such beliefs indicates that they fill important needs, and are worthy of objective study (Attridge, 2009). A paradox is that as a species, it seems we need to have faith in religious beliefs, yet also doubt their veracity. Science stimulates doubt and investigation, yet religious beliefs stimulate stability and sense of well-being. Is it possible to live like there is a transcendent being and at the same time doubt its existence? Can we have it both ways?

Despite current attempts to reconcile the conflicts between science and religion, the chasm continues to grow. Science has given us knowledge about our environment that has improved health and longevity, provided marvelous technology, and produced unparalleled comforts. This is not enough, though, for thinking humans. They also want knowledge about where they came from, why they are here, and where they are going, a release from the uncertainties of life. Psychologists such as Robert Emmons (1999) use the term, "ultimate concerns," but a more descriptive term reflecting the innate need for explaining existence is "ontological imperative" (see Chapter 2). People are uncomfortable with uncertainty, want a feeling of control and predictability, and have a natural tendency to attribute cause to observed phenomena (Heider 1944). Science reveals information about these things for phenomena that can be studied objectively with results that are replicable and agreed to by all observers (consensual validation), but science cannot answer questions about ultimate concerns because they are beyond the reach of objective research. Religion, on the other hand, directly answers these ultimate questions by organizing information about subjective experience, revelation, insight, and faith in a useful way.

Conflict occurs when science produces conclusions contrary to those previously established by religion. For some religious people this is either explained away or ignored, but for others it interferes with their commitment. For non-religious people, skepticism is heightened. Although psychology as a science has not been able to study the nature of ultimate reality, the object of the ontological imperative, it can study reactions and impacts. Much has been published about the sociology and psychology of religion, however little objective information is available about the growing population alienated from traditional religion but still concerned about ultimate reality beyond the reach of science.

Research at St Louis University (Wheeler, 2019) indicates that the nature of ultimate reality is not as important as the view that people have about it, and that a relationship exists between that view and an individual's health, well-being, and performance. It is possible that life may not have a purpose or underlying meaning, but we seem to have a need to believe it has. This view was described by Dr Wheeler as "life-esteem," a person's concept of ultimate reality, of purpose and meaning in life. The nature of ultimate reality seems to be obscure and controversial at the present time, but views and impacts that people have of it are more assessable. Life-esteem is a psychological term that can be investigated, and its impact can be objectively studied and usefully applied.

Religion

Concern with questions posed by the ontological imperative about ultimate reality was described in Chapter 4 as spirituality. It develops early in life and incorporates early learning, cultural influences, and ideas of others that seem to have more insight and knowledge. As social animals (Aronson, 1972), people tend to accept beliefs of their own social group that traditionally rely mainly on mystical subjective experience for justification. When a personal concept is developed well enough to form belief and to be shared with others, it becomes religion. Religion is defined here as a shared belief system that answers ultimate questions of the ontological imperative and usually provides for a transcendent force or supernatural being that has influenced or is influencing existence.

Since religion becomes a social enterprise, it takes on accouterments of social structure. Leaders emerge that vie for power, hierarchy is established with rank, and unquestionable dogma is formed. Organization results in churches, synagogues, temples, mosques, etc. that assume the role of spiritual care giver and ultimate authority with politics and power. The earliest known systems, based on animism, placed explanation and power in forces of nature and related deities, and relied on the good will of those mystical forces together with personal instincts and insights for sustenance, health, and well-being. As experience developed physical explanations and greater personal control of nature, people became less dependent on mystical sources; mystery decreased; personal power increased; and the belief systems became diverse and complex until at the present time there are thousands of religious belief systems. Respected leaders emerged. Shamans with special insight and access to nature and supernature gave way to priests with special connections to God, who in turn gave way to preachers and leaders that had special insight and knowledge about God. Most of the major current organizations are follow-ons to systems started long ago by brilliant charismatic leaders and have become institutionalized into a social structure. The structure claims exclusive validity about the ultimate cause of existence and explanation of what is still mysterious that increasingly conflicts with research findings, objective analysis, and personal experiences in the modern world.

There are many systems of traditional religions, and most have objects of devotion and worship, tenets of faith, and procedures of prayer that have many similarities as well as differences. It seems that the ultimate concerns of humans involve an innate universal need for devotion, faith, and prayer that develop into systems and organizations according to social interactions and benefits. Because of the abstract elusive nature of these ultimate concerns, they become represented by symbols, allegories, and anthropomorphisms (human characteristics) that can more easily be grasped and used. A feature of Christianity is the incarnation of God in Jesus, a human form of God that can be more meaningful than God as the "great I am." Although these representations facilitate the use of abstract concepts, when combined with emotional reactions and cognitive expediency they frequently become substitutes as idols and icons that obscure underlying concepts. For many people this fits in with the acceptance of dogma and authority of traditional religion. But, for others, such acceptance is not satisfying and spirituality as a more basic generic form of religion dominates. A person may accept the comforts of religion without being consciously aware of the pangs of doubt, however lurking somewhere is the individual's naturally occurring predisposition of spirituality, concern about the unknown. As Daniel Helminiak (1998) ably explained, it is an unavoidable consequence of being human.

Where traditional religion does not fill the ontological imperative, other systems develop. Some, such as Freemasonry reflect a progressive search; some, such as Nightingale-Conant focus on self-help; and some, such as Rosicrucian use ancient mysticism. A proliferation of quasi-religious organizations has come and gone, and at the present time there are many that exist as business enterprises under the guise of both commercial and non-profit organizations. Many use pseudo-scientific information to bolster their philosophy; most use self-help techniques; but all capitalize on the human restlessness and longing for satisfying answers to their questions of ultimate concern. The popularity of books and magazines about spirituality and religious mysticism attest to the growing dissatisfaction with mainstream belief systems, and the yearning for more explanations. It is important to recognize the role of science in this process, and sufficient information is now available to scientifically study religion and spirituality. Objective science cannot answer questions about ultimate reality as does religion, however many attempts are now succeeding to objectively study the subjective and anomalous phenomena on which religion and spirituality are based.

Science

Psychology, as an objectively oriented study of human nature, has supported the concept of needs to usefully account for the beliefs, attitudes, and values that result in the actions and reactions of both individuals and societies. For example, M.D. Faber (2004) has recently built the case supporting God as filling our need for the "great mysterious caregiver" that we all had as infants, but then lost as we learned about our existence. Prominent among the needs of people that have been supported by research or clinical experience are: understanding and predictability (George Kelly, 1955), community belonging (Alfred Adler, 1973), controllability (Julian Rotter, 1975), object of authority and worship (Erich Fromm, 1973), transcendent functioning (Carl Jung, 1938), religious sentiment (Gordon Allport. 1950), and sense of purpose (Viktor Frankl. 1997). This latter need of a purpose that gives meaning to one's life is so strong and obtuse that it is usually met abstractly by attributing it to a mystical source.

Religion has been found to provide for these needs as well as for others such as social support, belongingness, acceptance, salvation, harmony, and aesthetics, but religion has also provided prejudice and discrimination, even wars and genocide. Furthermore, religion is usually based on faith in a belief system that has been given and must be accepted regardless of conflicts with experience, knowledge, or logic resulting in limiting further inquiry and intolerance of alternatives. And since most people are aware of conflicts between faith-based religion and science-history, another important need, coherence, is aggravated (Antonovsky, 1987). Coherence is the need to feel that life makes sense and conflicts are manageable and meaningful. Science may be seen as an attempt to find out more about God's creation, but scientific attempts to find out more about the nature of God or ultimate reality is frequently discouraged by traditional religion because it may decrease coherence and faith in church dogma.

By using an inductive or bottom-up approach, science investigates speculation and assumptions about observable and falsifiable phenomena and corrects those that are unsupported or faulty. (Falsifiable means capable of being disproven if wrong.) This eliminates investigation of ultimate concerns because they are not observable or falsifiable, leaving ultimate concerns to the vicissitudes of human interpretations. It is known now that many healings previously attributed to mystical divine intervention can be explained as the result of the body's extensive powers of generation and regeneration; that prayer and religious experience have physical effects shared with meditation and ascetic experience; and that church attendance independent of belief is related to better physical health (Comstock & Partridge, 1972). Many phenomena labeled as miracles that were previously explained by divine intervention and used to support belief have now been shown to be explainable as naturally occurring physical activity. New discoveries in physics and biology indicate a natural explanation for many "mind over matter" phenomena used to justify belief in divine power. Even a Creator as first cause is now unnecessary because of recent support in physics for multiple universes, cyclic universe, and infinite space, indicating the possible absence of "beginning" (Stephen, 2021).

We all have beliefs, and we all have faith. Both involve assumptions that certain things will happen in certain situations with sufficient consistency that we can manage our lives with an acceptable degree of coherence, predictability, and meaning (Chapter 5). Optimal certainty is provided by another thing we seem to have: the built-in need to believe that there is something that is transcendent to, bigger and better than ourselves that got things started and that provided meaning and benevolent consistency. An ultimate goal is to strive for knowledge about this "something." Aggregation and elaboration of beliefs about it have created religions and institutions that have a "something" such as God based on subjective insight and revelation offering not only explanation of existence, but also offering comfort of an esoteric transcendent existence instead of the abyss of nothingness and futility of life's struggles. Increasingly, though, the dogma and revelations of religion conflict with objectively based information and experience.

Belief in a deity such as God can be vulnerable when based solely on religious revelation or faith. Current media coverage and emphasis on rationality magnifies inconsistencies between religious beliefs on one hand, and newly available information, relatively objective analysis, and logical reasoning on the other hand. Likewise, belief in a leader such as Jesus is more solid when based on historical information about that person's life, teachings, and legitimization of mystical phenomena, rather than solely on revelation or faith in handed down stories that could be myths. Joseph Campbell (1988) showed how myths can form a basis for beliefs or develop from beliefs to such an extent that they become vehicles that perpetuate and enhance their own power similar to what are now called "memes," culturally established concepts that continue because of their social momentum rather than objective logic (Dawkins, 2006). This does not mean that faith in religious dogma and writings are incorrect or unimportant. For many people it is insufficient to negate belief, but for many others it must be augmented with other moral, social, emotional, or objective factors to be sensible and retain validity. Are recognition of the positive factors and use of them to meet needs sufficient to justify such belief when considering conflicting factors?

Science provides revelations differently from religion in that they are tested for replicability and consensual validation in an attempt to separate them from faulty mental confabulation and irresponsible speculation. It has been well established that in interpreting sensory input the human mind modifies, augments, and reduces that input to such an extent that perception can be a distorted view of what is really out there. It is also well established that the human mind has great powers to manufacture perceptions that appear as insightful revelations but are merely amalgamations of information (both valid and invalid) already stored in the mind and frequently the result is a disjointed faulty conclusion. Research started by Elizabeth Loftus (1997) demonstrates the creativity and questionable accuracy of human memory. Neurological studies of meditation, prayer, awe, and sensory alteration started by Andrew Newberg and Eugene D'Aquili (2001) revealed that during such activities a common mechanism in the brain diminishes activity in centers of external orientation and increases activity in centers of internal attention and emotions, indicating that such activities may be accompanied with a loss of objective logic.

Writings such as those in the Bible, Koran, Torah, and Course in Miracles are examples of products that came mysteriously from human minds, and although they were inspired and contain inspiring passages with beneficial guidance, they are the interpretations of a human mind (or minds) and not necessarily direct information from a divine source. So, it seems appropriate to test revelation and faith and be aware of their foundations. Trouble and damaging conflict continue because of uncritical acceptance of interpretations of some passages in writings attributed to divine sources that require unquestioning faith, and aggressive imposition of those beliefs on other people.

Why then, do the religious beliefs that so effectively fill important needs become so narrowly focused that consideration and tolerance of alternatives is reduced to such an extent that the striving process to seek understanding and coherence is frustrated and damaging conflict occurs? The most viable answer to these questions is simply, human nature – it is the way we are, either as we were created or as we have evolved. In any case it seems to be built into our personality characteristics and is of increasing interest for both research and application. A volume edited by Harold Attridge (2009) provides a good summary of the debate that has been going on for many years about conflict between science and religion and the impact of that conflict on society.

The Great Paradox

As belief becomes a social enterprise reinforced by dogma, scriptures, revelation, and ritual requiring acceptance as a religion, doubt is many times driven into the dormant recesses of the subconsciousness mind. The belief then, as part of an established religion, is not questioned; and because of its nature, its foundation cannot be objectively investigated for falsification or objective support. The provisions of faith-based religions offer many comforts and benefits; however, the beliefs they require may be unsatisfactory from an objective logical viewpoint. Furthermore, as knowledge of the world increases and provides physical explanations that conflict with the dogma, more doubt occurs that if not a conscious issue, may be repressed and form a subconscious pocket of internal energy. The dogma must be accepted fully for pangs of doubt to be completely subdued. But doubt cannot be completely eliminated because of its role in stimulating science that has advanced civilization and provided the amazing material resources that we enjoy. These conflicts make traditional religion unsatisfactory for many people; but, on the other hand, science is also unsatisfactory because observation cannot reach out far enough to answer ultimate questions. A "great paradox" is that both are needed: science based on questioning and search, and religion based on faith and acceptance. The famous physicist Albert Einstein (1994, p.48) recognized this by saying "Science without religion is lame, religion without science is blind."

So, the provision for ultimate reality from religion becomes questionable, while that of science is incomplete. Neither by itself provides satisfactory answers to the questions posed. Combining religion and science has the potential of forming complete answers; however, this has not occurred in the past, and the current state of our human cognitive abilities indicates it will not happen in the near future. Thus, the need for both perpetuates the great paradox. Human nature dislikes paradox and tends to align with one side of the conflict to reduce dissonance. This produces a "great dilemma." The dilemma is that one feels that a choice must be made between belief and doubt, between search for truth or consolidation of faith. The result is an unsettling conundrum that needs to be recognized and considered.

Another conundrum that needs recognition is the "elusiveness paradox." This is the need to strive for a difficult or seemingly inaccessible goal. The nature of ultimate reality has been so elusive that it seems beyond our ability to grasp at the present time, and maybe never. But we cannot escape the need to continue in its search, even if the goal seems unattainable and the process is nebulous. What a difference our world would be if all societies recognized this situation and were oriented to this search instead of trying to impose a particular set of beliefs on others.

Although much has been written and said about ultimate reality and "theory of everything," none has emerged as being completely satisfactory. It seems that in our current state of intelligence and capability, they are inaccessible. Furthermore, the ugly possibility arises that there may not be an answer since history indicates that despite advances in knowledge about the material environment; no tangible progress has been made in knowledge of ultimate reality. Indeed, we seem to have regressed in our knowledge and use of a divine force that seemed to be active in earlier times. But the need is still so great that even though we cannot see the end goal and realize that it may be unattainable, we have an underlying need to continue the search.

Conciliation

So, how can traditional religion continue to meet the human need for belief and belonging, yet also satisfy the need for questioning and continuing quest? Some attempts are currently underway. Notable is the call of the Anglican priest and physicist John Polkinghorne (2007) for a "bottom-up" approach to theology. This bottom-up approach using science information to support reverence and belief in a sacred source has also been demonstrated by many other scientists such as Ursula Goodenough (1998), Candace Pert (2006), and Gary Schwartz (2006). Advocates of process theology, panentheism, theobiology, neurotheology, and others also contribute; however, conflicts still occur. In general, the conflicts start with the "top-down" approach of religion that then attempts to make the results compatible with scientific information, resulting in scientific minutia, philosophical obtuseness, or theological abstraction. As Donald Baxton (2007) points out, it becomes theology masquerading as academic inquiry.

The conflict occurs where the top-down deductive approach of religion intersects with the bottom-up inductive approach of science. The strict bottom-up approach publicized by Daniel Dennett (2006), Richard Dawkins (2006), Sam Harris (2004), Victor Stenger (2003), and others finds no support or need for metaphysical or supernatural explanations. It seems that the best way at the present time to minimize an oxymoron situation is to admit that the two approaches conflict, but both are needed because they represent separate domains of knowledge that contribute to civilization. Each has useful components beyond their intersection. The famous paleontologist and science educator Stephen Gould (2006) described this as "nonoverlapping magisteria."

Concepts of deity are limited only by imagination, and they are stimulated by a complex interaction of needs. The need of providing for the mysterious unknown can be conveniently met by accepting useful aspects of established beliefs and focusing on beneficial effects, however the unrelenting force of spirituality to question and continue search is in the background somewhere. For many people, the need to believe and accept appears stronger than the need for objective explanation. For others, the need for objective explanation dominates. However, for most, both are needed: a religion to believe in and an ultimate concern to pursue. Both approaches can be accepted as useful if the value of each is recognized.

By extending objective knowledge resulting from doubt with subjective meaning resulting from faith, there results a dialectic tension that energizes development and satisfies need for meaning and purpose. A belief built on knowledge acquired through observation, study, and experience is more secure than a belief based on revelation or dogma that has been handed down through teachings or scriptures. New information adds to the former but detracts from the latter. It can follow that there may really be some form of life beyond our knowledge, transcendent to our personal lives that could be regarded as a divine force—a deity that set-in motion the developing complexity of our world. At the present time, the true nature of this deity seems beyond our grasp. We have need to believe that there is such a transcendent force, while recognizing that such a belief may be speculation and worthy of doubt.

We are seekers and believers, so if we accept one and set aside the other, an unnatural repression occurs that can boil to the surface at an inappropriate time. If we can accept both, seeking can continue while the comforts of belief can be experienced without serious interruption.

The social psychologist David Meyers (2008) in his book *A Friendly Letter to Skeptics and Atheists,* proposed a usefulness for believing and doubting. He professes belief in Christianity based on passion rather than intellect; however, he justifies continuing prevalence of religious belief on its ability to fill human needs for social support, meaning, purpose, acceptance, and hope. He summarized the results of his experiences and research with the belief that "(1) there is a God and (2) it's not me (and it's not you) --- and that we should hold our own untested beliefs tentatively, assess other's ideas with open minded skepticism, and when appropriate, use observation and experimentation to winnow error from truth" (p. 4).

Conciliation of the conflict is possible with the potential of consilience for the long sought unifying theory proposed by sociobiologist E. O. Wilson (2006). Success in accepting and living with conflict rewards individuals with a feeling of emotional comfort as well as of progress and the satisfaction of pursuing a process leading toward a meaningful goal; and for societies, the reward is release from the competitive and violent efforts to impose one set of beliefs or interests on other people. The great dilemma could be eliminated, rewarding individuals and societies with a sense of coherence that unites pursuit of discovery with comforts and benefits of religious faith. Resolving these issues represent a major milestone toward developing an acceptable unified theory. Here are two suggestions for consideration.

Nognosticism

The first is to realize that we do not know fully the nature of Truth, first cause, or ultimate reality. A case has already been made to support the limitation of knowledge about our existence. We recognize that our knowledge and perceptions are limited and that there is more than what is in our current awareness. There must be something that caused our existence, some reason for it, and to be motivated to participate in it despite hardship and unpleasantness There seems to be something beyond our current knowledge, something transcendent to our personal lives that set-in motion the developing complexity of our world. This could be natural or supernatural. At the present time, it is highly questionable that anyone knows its true nature. We seem to have need to believe that there is a transcendent being, while recognizing that such a belief may be speculation and worthy of doubt.

It may be a thankless task to believe in a transcendent something yet continue to seek substantiation or alternatives that eliminate doubt and provide for ultimate reality. Agnosticism holds that it cannot be accomplished and dooms us to the fate of Sisyphus, the Greek king who was condemned by the God Zeus to spend eternity repeatedly carrying a large rock to the top of a high hill and watching it roll down (Camus 1960). But the continued advance of knowledge indicates that just because it is not now known, does not mean it is unknowable. This is "nognosticism," a term used here to represent an alternative to agnosticism, theism, and atheism. The nature of ultimate reality seems beyond our ability to grasp at the present time; but we cannot escape the need to continue in search, even if its goal seems inaccessible and its process becomes subjugated to belief (the elusiveness paradox).

Science and religion may converge some-day, but it will not be any time soon. In the meantime, for optimal well-being and health, we must recognize the need for both, and work toward the "great conciliation" of religion and belief vs. science and doubt, striving for a seemingly inaccessible goal while living in the world as it seems at the present time, here and now.

Ecumenical Humanism

The second suggestion is that while having belief in "our own system" we must recognize that it may not be the absolute Truth and we must be tolerant of other belief systems. Different societies have different needs ameliorated by different beliefs. The term "ecumenical humanism" implies a philosophy that places humans at the center of existence and sees them as holistic, self-determining, especially endowed organisms that are oriented toward a goal of continuing existence with development of knowledge, understanding, and mastery of nature. Humans are at the center because their minds know best their own perceptions. They have need for a belief system that provides an explanation of the unknown without dogmatic intolerance. Different religions fill this need for different people through different beliefs about some form of transcendent deity. For Christians this is God as manifest in Jesus Christ and as explained in the New Testament. To fit in with most Christian churches one must accept Jesus as the provider of all needs and the avenue to salvation after death. Other religions have even more stringent dogma that requires subjugating further inquiry to acceptance. Such acceptance stymies further search into the purpose and meaning of one's existence and life in general. In this case, Truth is not something to search for because it is revealed through faith, and faith results from acceptance of a particular belief system.

Many people have difficulty with suppression of the search for Truth and ultimate reality. Many people have not found any church or organized system that is satisfying. For them, belief in a transcendent being or force that provides for and explains existence by supplementing the limitations of science would be more satisfying if supported by consensual information, objective analysis, and logic rather than only by religious teachings of faith. A destiny seems to be for people to search either consciously or subconsciously. Teilhard de Chardin (1965) said this from a philosophical viewpoint, and Martin Seligman (2002) said this from a scientific viewpoint. Yes, revelation and faith are important; without them we would flounder in ambiguous solipsism (extreme egocentrism). But combining objective analysis with religious belief frequently results in conflicts and malaise. Commitment to a belief system is more satisfying if it can be accompanied by a feeling of coherence between its articles of faith and worldly experience.

People are so complex and sophisticated with ideas that result from such a complicated interaction of temperaments, experiences, values, attitudes, and beliefs, that spiritual ideas are rarely the same for any two individuals. Social interdependence brings people together into societies that stimulate the sharing and adjustment of personal ideas to produce organized group beliefs and culture. Such is the history of religion; but despite the universality of human needs and the desire of harmony and coherence, many different belief systems have been organized, each being useful for that particular social group. As used here, the term ecumenical humanism recognizes that each has reason for existence if it ameliorates the ontological imperative in a humanitarian way. This is a melding of secular humanism and religious theology.

Pragmatic Pluralism

Under what classification would be a belief system that accepts the probability of alternate transcendent realities beyond our present knowledge, that accepts the need to both believe and doubt the existence of a transcendent divinity, that accepts the need to search for ultimate reality, and that accepts the need for tolerating and cooperating with multiple seeking avenues while living constructively in the here and now? It would not be theism, deism, pantheism, or atheism; nor would it be panentheism, theological humanism, or religious naturalism, although they accept some aspects for these factors.

The term "pluralism" implies acceptance of multiple approaches and realities, and tolerance of alternate views and beliefs. The term "pragmatism" implies maintaining contact with needs of existence and well-being as they seem at the present time. So, maybe the term "pragmatic pluralism" would be acceptable to people aware of their need to believe in a divinity and share it with others; people who recognize that this belief may involve plural realities and that they are doomed to pursue knowledge of it while living pragmatically in the "here and now"; and people who are dissatisfied with the limitations, irrationalities, and conflicts of traditional beliefs. This is explained further in the next chapter.

Implications

As thinking humans, we are concerned with why we are here, where we came from, and where we are going, ultimate concerns. We recognize that our knowledge is limited and that there is a mysterious unknown that may contain reality, force, or divinity in a realm transcendent to our current knowledge. We need to believe there is such a transcendent realm, but any beliefs about its nature are questionable and should be held tentatively. We need both belief and doubt.

We cannot prove or disprove that there is something in the way of a supreme being or transcendent realm, and whether there is or is not, whether we believe or not, we should recognize the benefits of living as if there is. For social justice, we need a moral authority that transcends the vagrancies of human judgment. For personal coherence and happiness, we need the possibility that there is a cause that gives purpose and meaning for our existence. We need to think that there is something for us beyond just surviving physically. We need to feel that there is some way to atone for our missteps. We need to be conscious of our subconscious dependence on a mystical caregiver. We need an object of devotion and source of unconditional love. And finally, we need to recognize that we do not know everything, and that in the realm of the unknown anything may exist—even plural realties and the divine supreme being of our forefathers.

Religions have traditionally filled these needs, and some people are attracted to other organizations or movements because of the needs. People tend to subscribe to the most expedient belief system available, systems that develop a life of their own with leaders and activists that propel it to an elite status calling for supplication and faith. If people are aware of the origin of the system to which they are attracted, they can recognize the paradox, dilemma, and uncertainty involved and be tolerant of modifications and other proposed possibilities. Assertion and proselytization can give way to cooperation and development. Prejudice and conflict can give way to assistance and exchange. That is, if they can believe and doubt at the same time.

Chapter 7

Pragmatic Pluralism

A study of history and anthropology indicates that as far back as humans can be traced, they have had beliefs in supernatural powers. These beliefs grew out of the built-in need for meaning, manageability, and explanation for their lives—the ontological imperative introduced in Chapter 2. And these beliefs have been important in the development of civilization. Furthermore, a study of psychology, sociology, and neuroscience indicates that belief in supernatural power helps meet many important human needs such as meaning, purpose, social support, coherence, structure, acceptance, stable ethics, moral authority, and immortality. Anthropology and history indicate that such beliefs could have developed through adaptive evolution or could have been implanted by design (Szocik, 2017). Probably more important, though, is a study of recent findings from the physical sciences indicating that explanations of our universe and existence support theories such as many-worlds, cyclic-universe, multiverses, cosmic-consciousness, and supernatural-design (Stephen, 2021). This implies scientific support and natural explanation for many mystical phenomena that had been attributed to a supernatural realm in the past.

The popular theory of quantum mechanics developed in physics nicely explains observations of subatomic activity where particles are also waves that can exist in more than one place at the same time (superposition), that exist as multiple potentialities in a wave function until materialized (collapsed) by being observed or used, and once connected with another particle can communicate instantly (entangled) when separated from that once connected particle. Quantum mechanics opened the door for many interesting studies involving such things as consciousness and information being basic constituents of nature. Astrophysicist Bernard Haisch (2010) uses discoveries in physics to support an information system that is an intelligence underlying the universe, a form of consciousness or "great thought" that created reality. Physicist Evan Walker (2000, p. 326) proposed that our material universe results from the collapse of potentialities by a prehuman "quantum mind." He writes, "In the beginning was the Quantum Mind, a first cause, itself time independent and nonlocal, which created space-time and matter-energy." This could be called Supermind or even God as a Great Architect that started things. It also could be called Great Observer that not only started things but can intercede now at a quantum level. Thus, God could affect matter without violating physical laws.

The word atom comes from a Greek word meaning indivisible. Less than a hundred years ago the atom was considered the smallest object in nature. It could not be further reduced. However, as researchers peered into the nature of atoms and developed techniques for looking closer into their structure (microcosm), more was observed. Eventually atoms were found to be made up of sophisticated classes of particles and forces called fermions and bosons such as quarks, leptons, photons, and gluons. Furthermore, it seems that these basic particles and forces consist of energy that in turn consist of something more basic such as relationships, information, or intelligence (Kuhlmann, 2013). As research continues other particles and forces are being found indicating that there is more to be found. The variety of subatomic constituents are limited only by the ability to observe them or their effects. (More about this is in Chapter 14.)

Similar results occur for the researchers that study outer space (macrocosm), in that the limits of space are a function of the distance that can be observed. Albert Einstein explained the observed limits of space as the result of space curving back onto itself. These limits have now been expanded to include dark matter, dark energy, and black holes with the possibility of multiple universes. We exist in the one that happens to have conditions that support our form of life (Davies, 2008). In other universes there may be different forms of life and different laws of nature—alternate realities.

Since the limits of the microcosm and the macrocosm expand with the expansion of observational capabilities, a logical conclusion can be made that space and time go on and on, maybe even to infinity. The concept of infinity is difficult to grasp, because within the realm of infinity not only could anything exist, but somewhere everything would exist. This would include unknown forces, spirits, souls, and deities that may exist in alternate realities as well as in unknown aspects of our natural reality. This implies a pluralism of realities beyond our known physical world, beyond the popular dualism of physical-mental. Such pluralism implies that unknown things may exist in our natural reality as well as in other possible realities. Anything is therefore possible, even the Gods of our forefathers.

But in the meantime, we exist in a physical world whose nature we can know best through our sensory perceptions that are influenced by expectations, wishes, and beliefs that many times distort our view. Our uniquely human emotions produce feelings both good and bad that sometimes provide experiences with fleeting glimpses of an unknown realm, a realm indicating existence of a possible alternate reality with an environment different (metaphysical) or beyond (supernatural) our own. Unfortunately, these experiences are too ephemeral for practical use and reliable benefit. Greatest well-being seems to result from objective attempts to harness and use our known physical environment while pursuing metaphysical possibilities—striving to know the unknown while effectively using what is known.

This is where pragmatism enters. Even though anything is possible, we must live with what is happening here and now and with our view of what will probably occur. What is useful and practical comes best by being respectful of and searching for the unknown while living effectively with what is known. Such efforts have the probability of providing an uplifting sense of meaning and purpose that energizes our daily struggles for existence. It is important that we recognize useful reliable information about our situation and use it to live effectively in the "here and now" without suppression from unyielding ideology, the sacrifice of personal belief, or of being diverted by speculative possibilities and fear of uncertainty.

The term "pragmatic pluralism" has been used loosely over the years by philosophers attempting to apply the metaphysical approach to the varied human perspectives on value, ethics, and religion as proposed by William James (2006). This is explained by the notable Finnish philosopher Sami Pihlstrom in his 2013 book, *Pragmatic*

Pluralism and the Problem of God. My book, *Mountains and Minds*. published in 2010 established a formal definition of pragmatic pluralism as a practical theory of life that recognizes the possibility of alternate realities while living effectively in the world as it now presents itself. This theory was supported in *Mountains and Minds* with what was considered scientific information and it was proposed as a foundation for a religious belief that makes sense with personal experience, and reliable information. It is an alternative to theism that requires unquestioned faith in a specific supernatural deity, atheism that is belief that there can be no supernatural deity, and agnosticism that believes there probably is a supernatural deity, but its nature is impossible to know. Pragmatic pluralism admits that the "if and what" of deity is currently inconclusive, but a belief in some form of deity is needed, and with further development the unknown and uncertainty will decrease. If societies were oriented toward a joint pursuit of such development instead of competing for ideologically based dominance, much violence and terrorism would be replaced with cooperation and tolerance.

Pragmatic pluralism is a philosophy of life or worldview recognizing that anything is possible creating a mysterious unknown realm, but that not everything is probable, and that it is best to live in the "here and now" as the world presents itself while pursuing knowledge of this mysterious realm. It supports a belief in something transcendent to our personal self that provides meaning and purpose for our existence, and that since we are uncertain of its nature, we are destined to search for knowledge of it and tolerate alternate approaches. Because of varied make-up and experience, we all have varied ideas about this philosophy and live with interpretations most useful and sensible to us individually. The resulting belief would then fit in with science, experience, and religion, and be a believable belief. Much anxiety and depression would be reduced if people were more aware of this philosophy, and if society emphasized it along with the current emphasis on physical resources and entertainment.

Chapter 8

Thinking, Believing, and Feeling

A major part of daily life is making decisions and judgements, and the major ways this is done can be grouped into thinking, believing, and feeling. It may be a combination of these, but usually one method dominates. I think it is going to rain tomorrow because the weather report shows a cold front approaching with high moisture content and low barometric pressure. I believe it is going to rain tomorrow because John Fuller said so on TV and I have faith in his prediction. I feel it is going to rain tomorrow because of an intuitive hunch or foreboding; I feel it in my bones. Wow, which one of these ways of drawing a conclusion is best? One is an effortful thinking process using information; one is fast and convenient using acceptance of authority; and the last one is a fast and convenient reaction of subjective feeling and insight.

We all use each of these methods at different times, but how often do we question the validity of their results? By far the most accurate is thinking when reliable information and time for analysis are available. But thinking requires conscious time-consuming effort while belief and feeling produce fast reactions not requiring conscious thinking. Psychologists have found that despite our emphasis on deliberate thinking, most of our actions and reactions are subconsciously determined without much conscious thought (Braisby, 2012). Thinking is most reliable, but it may not be best if reliable information is not available or if fast response is needed not allowing time for thought processes to take place. Your fast reaction that hands a twenty-dollar bill to a friend asking for donation to a Christian missionary may be an example of decision based on feeling about your friend's effort, or it may be because of your Christian belief that supports missionaries. Yet, taking time to get information about the missionary and thinking about values may have concluded that the money would be better used by your community food drive for local people.

A fast reaction can also be a reflex involving subconscious processes linking sensory input to nerve components that control muscle action bypassing conscious mental processes of thinking. Similarly, fast emotional reaction from feeling usually uses a subconscious mental process with intuition, instinct, and insight that by-pass conscious thought. In between the two extremes of thinking and feeling is faith in a belief that likewise short cuts laborious thinking processes and is more reliable than hunches from feeling. This is a conclusion from prior thinking or experience, or a conclusion accepted from social influence. Spiritual beliefs associated with religion are an important example of stored information that affects decisions. Belief is a conclusion drawn from prior thinking, experience, and learning that is especially influenced by society and early childhood experiences.

Experiences that have been forgotten by our conscious mind may linger in subconscious memory and be triggered by a current situation. The smell of alcohol may trigger memories of that unpleasant time in the doctor's office when that cut was being sewed up and may now produce an irrational fear when using an alcohol hand sanitizer. How many times have you had an unexplained feeling that influenced your action or reaction and then wondered, why did I do that? Both beliefs and feelings are powerful motivators, and since they usually result from memories and physiological reaction beyond awareness and conscious thought, they may cause inappropriate action. Unfortunately, our process of interpreting a situation and reacting either by beliefs or feelings is not perfect. Consequently, we sometimes take actions that later we realize were not the best (Wheeler, 2019).

Where do these beliefs and feelings come from and how reliable are they? One source is direct experience by which we learn first-hand information pertaining to particular situations. Since I hit my sister because she was bugging me and I got severely punished, I refrain now from hitting my sister when she bugs me. Another source is vicarious learning when we receive information from parents, teachers, and media through observation. When I see my brother severely punished for hitting my sister, I also refrain from hitting her. All our experiences affect learning, particularly when they involve family, friends, culture, or a transcendent source as provided by most religions. Furthermore, it has been found that the sources do not necessarily have to be respected, because mere exposure can plant enduring memories, especially if they are related to strong emotions. Previous learning and experience are stored in memory to form beliefs that help trigger feelings later.

It must be recognized that sometimes a person's actions, reactions, and decisions defy normal thinking, believing, or feeling. The human mind has great powers of confabulation; that is, it can select, modify, and generate information with odd results. Furthermore, chemical ingestions, expectations, or brain functioning problems can produce odd results. These conditions are beyond the scope here, but the possibility of such conditions producing either valid or invalid insight cannot be ruled out.

For life to be meaningful and manageable, people need belief that events affecting them have sufficient reliability to provide predictable outcomes, that there is a purpose for their daily endeavors, and that there is a reliable source beyond the vicissitudes and vagrancies of human judgments. Physiological make-up and learning form information stored in the brain for use in thinking, or for forming beliefs and feelings. Thinking uses the stored information directly for analytical results when time permits, whereas beliefs use previously established conclusions, and feelings use previously established reactions. Acting or reacting with thinking requires more effort and time than with believing or feeling but are usually more reliable.

Cultures are built on concerns about the source and nature of these processes, and the concerns have stimulated a searching for information that has developed amazing technology producing unparalleled comfort, convenience, and healthfulness; but questions linger about sources and nature of these processes. John Fuller's weather prediction may fail after that cold front arrives; sometimes it does not rain when my barometer needle drops; and sometimes it does not rain despite my strong hunch. The search for making good decisions continues, but elusiveness challenges thinking, requires assumptions and speculation, and encourages dogmatic belief. Reliance on authority supports beliefs, and emotional reaction supports feelings of knowing, resulting in many benefits such as fast response, release from the discomfort of uncertainty, and management of conflict; but they are sometimes inappropriate.

As knowledge increases, new information may conflict with previously established beliefs and feelings of knowing to such an extent that accuracy of all beliefs and feelings become questionable. Believing and feeling are each important for effective living. But also, for effective living, these processes should be flexible enough to accommodate new knowledge and experience, and thus be free of serious doubt. It is useful to review one's beliefs and feelings at appropriate times and make modifications if needed. If you have reviewed your feelings and beliefs, and found them compatible with your current situation, knowledge, and experience, you can be confident in your decisions, choices, and actions. Your life will be meaningful and manageable even in the face of adversity, and it will be free of debilitating uncertainty.

Chapter 9

The Need for God?

The term *Anthropocene* is now being used to define a geological period when a major influence on the Earth's environment is human activity. Within the last one thousand (or so) years humans have occupied and proliferated in most areas of the Earth taxing the Earth's ability to support the increasing population. Furthermore science, engineering, and technology have allowed human activity to establish control over many functions previously controlled only by nature or supernature. Much of our environment is now the result of human activity. We no longer are completely dependent on natural or supernatural forces to control the environment; we no longer seem to be helplessly dependent on either nature or supernature.

The human propensity to exist and reproduce has always propelled ingenuous ways to explain and influence the environment. In early days, the best explanation was a mysterious power, and the best way for influence was supplication and appeal to that power. Belief in mysterious power led to social acceptance of various forms of supernatural deity. Thus, religions evolved that dominated social groups providing not only explanations but also codes of conduct, salvation, support, comfort, belonging, meaning, and purpose. But, with recent scientific advances these benefits were available without use of supernatural force. Morality and codes of conduct became established more by human acclaim (either democratic or dictatorial) rather than revelation, and sustenance came more from ingenuity and productivity rather than solely from prayer and supplication.

Civilization has advanced with the availability of unparalleled health, comfort, and longevity. Humans have learned that the absolute authority of ancient religions can be violated without immediate punishment, and that science gives more useful explanations of environmental happenings than does religion. Liberalism has released society from imposed respect of conservatism and allowed authority and morality to be determined by human judgements and politics. Despite these advances though, major problems exist.

Ideologies of religion are now used to justify political domination and violence, and have become ineffective in reigning in harmful activities previously repressed more effectively. Many people are now turned off from traditional religion because of conflict with science and personal experiences. Yes, we need a belief in a deity such as God. But it must be belief that makes sense with current day happenings and reliable findings of science. How can that be acquired and benefits of religion preserved?

First, we must have a God that provides a "first cause" without illogical characteristics. We live in a cause-and-effect environment and now that we have more leisure time, we dig deeper into questions that lead to ultimate cause—what started things. It must be something beyond our observable world, something transcendent to our physical experiences. This may be a Supermind that caused collapse of the wave function in quantum mechanics, or an unknowable Force behind all creation, or maybe Creation itself. Human society has always been dominated by belief in some form of such power, but it needs to eliminate much of the illogical baggage it has now acquired.

Second, we must have a God that supports our needs for existence and continuance. This is the God we seem to have developed. As humans have develop through evolutionary adaption, the concept emerged of a God that would provide first cause, explanation of existence, and meet other human needs such as meaning and purpose of existence, moral authority, immortality, forgiveness, acceptance, and unconditioned love. This God may have supernatural powers even though it may have emerged from human cognitive creativity to meet needs. This is the pragmatic God recently proposed by the astrophysics author, Nancy Adams (2015) as the "God that can be real," in the face of recently shaken dogmas of religion. Since this God grew out of sophisticated human needs, its nature would not conflict with knowledge and experience, but it would require acceptance of a paradox involving a supernature that emerged from nature. As bold as this is, it is not new. Voltaire in 1770 wrote, "If God did not exist, it would be necessary to invent him" (Bartlett, 1967, p.325).

Third, we need a metaphorical God that represents the order, mystery, and creativity of our environment. This would be a representation of a mysterious God that can be easily grasped. It would be a symbol of ultimate reality that could be referred to without encumbrances of dogmatic beliefs that conflict with knowledge and experience. This God can be trusted, worshipped, and provides the benefits of traditional religion without illogical supernatural beliefs. Symbols and icons can make this metaphorical representation more meaningful and easier to grasp. Rituals and ceremonies can be more meaningful and enjoyable.

So, maybe we need three Gods. One with supernatural power that came first and created our world and may continue to influence it. One that was created by humans to meet needs and emerged with supernatural power. And one that is a metaphorical symbol representing that allusive ultimate reality from which humans developed that can be easily grasped and that provides benefits of religion without illogical beliefs. Could they all be the same? Could they all result from a deity that set-in motion development of the human species and civilization? Or could they result from a deity that set-in motion the process that developed an emergent God? Or could they be different aspects of an ultimate reality? We do not know for sure, but together they support a worldview that promotes respect for constructive activities that sustain and perpetuate existence. Any of the Gods could be actual or they could be symbols of a power that provides the benefits of traditional religion. It would be nice if our media, politician, and educators emphasized these issues rather than the consumerism, power plays, and conflicts with which we are currently dominated. Cooperation and construction could replace violence and destruction.

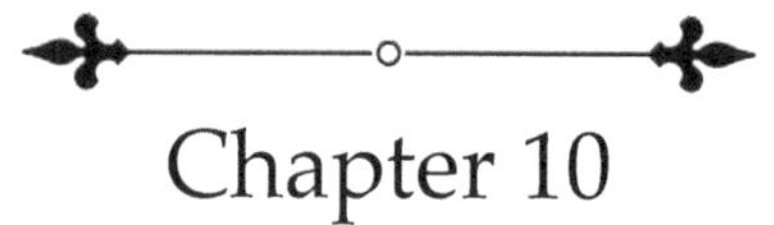

Chapter 10

Happiness and Flourishing

We all want to be happy, to feel good, to have enjoyment. And most of us spend much effort in pursuing those things. But how successful are these efforts? Do you really feel better when you finish watching that show? After the diversion, are your problems still causing a nagging stress? Our comforts and the time devoted to entertainments and pleasure are at an historic high, yet depression, anxiety, and suicide are also at historic highs. Maybe there is something more that will make the temporary good feeling more lasting.

New research indicates that those people reporting a high level of happiness do not pursue happiness directly but experience it as a by-product of things they do that have a focus outside of themselves (Smith, 2017). These are things like doing well at work, teaching a child to read, or participating in a charitable organization This idea is not new. It was in the fifth century BCE when the term eudaimonia was used to describe a happy purposeful philosophy of life (Flanagan, 2009).

The philosophy of hedonia also originated in ancient fifth century Greece when Aristippus emphasized that the purpose in life is to experience personal pleasure. Epicurus broadened this philosophy to justify self-centered lifestyles. Aristotle, on the other hand, proposed eudaimonia as the philosophy that there is more to life than pursing personal pleasure and immediate gratification. The purpose in life is to use one's talents effectively and focus on something outside of oneself. The famous philosopher Owen Flanagan (2009) described this as flourishing—living the good life.

Two things have brought flourishing to the feature page. One is the realization that despite the advances in comfort, health, and technology; depression, anxiety, and suicide seem to be increasing while happiness is not likewise increasing. Second is a reorientation of psychology research started by Martin Seligman in 1998. This was a shift from emphasis on causes and treatment of mental problems to causes and avenues for good mental health—that is, development of resilience, fortitude, energy, and happiness.

Emily Smith in her book The *Power of Meaning* (2017) summarizes this trend in psychology research and points out that the efforts have focused on studies of happiness. She lays a foundation for increased emphasis on a neglected factor in these happiness studies. This is sense of meaning in one's activities and life that is associated with a sense of purpose.

This, too, is not a new idea. Just after World War II the famous Austrian psychiatrist, Viktor Frankl (1997), popularized the concept of "purpose-in-life." He showed that a major cause of depression and anxiety was a person's feeling of a lack of purpose in activities and life. Since such feeling drains happiness from one's life, developing a sense of purpose should provide meaning and happiness to his psychiatric patients and he instigated a remedy called logotherapy. This has been broadened as a mental health topic useful not only for patients, but also for average people to alleviate anomie, sadness, lethargy, and burnout. Psychologist Robert Emmons (1999) adds a particular goal of searching for the whys and wherefores of existence, what he calls ultimate concerns, as being related to health, well-being, and performance. The book, *Climbing Higher* (Wheeler, 2019) summarizes research indicating that for one's sense of purpose to produce sufficient meaning to influence lasting happiness, it needs to have goals of increasing understanding of the cause and nature of existence (whys and wherefores) and improving human civilization (contribution). These goals are so long-range that they are never completely met and provide meaning and sense of purpose on a continuing basis. The purpose is something beyond meeting immediate needs or pursuing short-range goals. These goals and ways of pursuing them may not be clear but searching for them may be a more beneficial goal in itself.

Psychologist Roy Baumeister (2005) who has spent many years studying meaning stated that pursuit of happiness that ignores meaning and purpose is likely to fail (more on this in Chapter12). In his 2011 book, *Flourish,* psychologist Martin Seligman pointed out that direct pursuit of happiness may be successful, but the result is fleeting and many times counterproductive. It can be concluded that authentic lasting happiness is a by-product of doing things on a continuing basis that fit in with a long-range idealistic purpose outside of oneself focused on ultimate concerns and human advancement. Much of the current problems of today would be alleviated if our media, politicians, and educators would emphasize the role of this sense of purpose and stimulate investigation of its nature rather than emphasizing more immediately available personal pleasures, entertainment, gratification, and power.

The Good Life

Achieving happiness is now associated with having a "good life." It seems to be the product of a sophisticated brain process that seeks good ways to exist and answers to "big questions" such as why I am here and what am I doing? To have these things people developed customs, ethics, ideologies, and religions that have been driving forces in the development of civilization. Aristotle described this effort as "eudaimonia," but a more recent term now in use is "flourishing" (Seligman, 2011). Health and well-being of both individuals and societies are now recognized as requiring more than just meeting daily needs. What is needed for this good life beyond the physical requirements of daily existence?

In addition to feeling that personal existence is manageable and secure, people need a sense of purpose oriented to something beyond themselves, something that gives constructive meaning to activities, a striving for something bigger or higher than personal comfort, and a search for answers to big questions. It seems that all humans have these needs built into them. Whether these needs evolved through adaption to requirements of existence or were implanted by a creator is not as important as recognizing that they exist in all normally functioning humans These "ultimate concerns" about "whys and wherefores" are not as pressing as meeting immediate needs of daily life, so they may be pushed aside out of consciousness awareness. Our culture even encourages this by emphasizing "getting and spending." The struggle to meet daily needs and for wealth, power, and success many times leaves little room for pursuing nebulous deep explanations. This goal is still there, though, and may surface in times of crisis, or it may surface as an unsettled feeling of dissatisfaction. Seeking answers is an "ontological imperative" (Chapter2) because it is an unavoidable concern about fundamental being (ontos from ancient Greece) that is the essence of "spirituality" (Chapter 4). It is a desire to reach out to something beyond our activities of daily life, to climb higher and to access the good life. My research in psychology shows that such spirituality is a personality trait that exists in everyone but manifest in varying degrees and ways (Wheeler, 2019) (see Chapter 4).

Spirituality as defined here has been a dominant force throughout known human history. It started either through revelation or through mundane attempts to explain important phenomena and was a basis for development of religions, culture, and civilizations. Because natural explanations of ultimate concerns were not available in ancient times, supernatural ones were frequently invoked. As these were shared with other people and reinforced, they took on structure and beliefs forming religions that still dominate societies.

Religions became social enterprises that filled many important needs, not only explanation of mysteries, but also physical and mental support, acceptance and positive regard, belongingness and social identity, and salvation from nothingness. These benefits required belief and faith in established concepts that became dogma. As knowledge increased and science developed, natural explanations conflicted with dogma causing doubts about many supernatural beliefs. Doubt about faith-based explanations has been a driving force for scientific and technological advances producing the comforts and capabilities that we now enjoy. However, this has undermined traditional religion and reduced much of religions benefits for many people. A "great paradox" is that both are needed: faith and belief in a transcendent explanation of ultimate concerns that cannot be provided by science, and questioning that stimulated science whose explanations undermined benefits of religion. (explained in Chapter 6.) It is important to recognize and accept the great paradox in order to be prepared for the dilemma and uncomfortable uncertainty it may cause. Since people try to avoid uncertainty, they tend to choose one side of a dilemma, making prior beliefs stronger and intolerant of alternatives.

So, the good life can be fostered by recognizing importance of the ontological imperative and the paradox, dilemma, and uncertainty that result. It stimulates our vitality and is a driving force for the continued advance of civilization. A personal view of this is spirituality (Chapter 4) that varies among people, and when shared with other people it becomes religion that varies among societies. Various views exist more because they meet needs rather than being right or wrong. So, we must be tolerant of other beliefs without sacrificing our own. We must recognize that at the present time our view is limited and that beyond that view anything could exist, but at the present time beliefs about what is out there should be held tentatively. Although anything could be possible, not everything is probable, and we must live in the world as it presents itself to us "here and now," a view of existence that could be called "pragmatic pluralism" (Chapter 7).

Thinking along these lines would orient people toward the good life and stimulate lasting happiness. How nice it would be if our media, politicians, and educators would emphasize these fundamental issues rather than crime, power, and violence. For individuals it would decrease anxiety, depression, and confusion. For societies it would decrease conflict, terrorism, and aggression.

Chapter 11

Personal and Social Flourishing

Many people wonder about why they do the things they do, what is the purpose of their activities, what is the purpose of their life. Answers usually list first, to existence and to improve fitness for existence. Number two is continuation of existence which in a biological sense means reproduction, sex. Third is flourishing which means feeling good about what they are doing. And then comes autonomy, the freedom to do what they desire. The way they want to do things frequently conflicts with the way they are allowed to do them. Why are there so many laws, rules, regulations, and expectations that constrain their freedom and creativity? Why the big conflict between free enterprise and socialism, between personal freedom and social constraint, and between individualism and communalism?

The answer is that they are not alone. If everyone went to work only when they wanted to, business would fall apart. If everyone did only what they wanted, we would live in chaos. We all recognize that constrictions are necessary for our lives with others to be manageable. Throughout known history, a major issue has been the conflict between short-term personal desires and long-term social desires—individualism vs communalism. This is a major cause of dissatisfaction, anxiety, and depression that interferes with a meaningful flourishing life for many people (Seligman, 2011).

We are social animals (Aronson, 1972). No animal is more dependent on the fellow members of its species than humans. We spend more time in childhood and elderly years dependent on caregivers than any other species. Throughout human history there has always been some form of social structure that facilitated reciprocal benefits among individuals. At the most primitive level it was provided by family with a patriarch or matriarch. Families merged into tribes with a chieftain or council and then into nations and empires with emperors, kings, rulers. and presidents. Many different types of government have been used, none of which were able to maintain a satisfactory balance between personal freedom and communal welfare.

A major reason for difficulties in this issue is human nature, the huge variance in capabilities of individuals to meet the needs of existence. Physical and mental abilities of some extend their years of dependency and they need help from those with greater ability. People with greater ability tend to revel with their power, while those of lesser ability have a tendency to expect entitlements. Psychology studies characteristics of individuals and their personal functioning, and sociology studies how people form societies and function in groups. As societies develop, their structures become complicated enough to support studies of other fields such as political science and government. Massive structures have developed in societies to constrain personal freedom of individuals.

The most ideal structure theoretically for a social group is probably socialism where a central government manages affairs of the society for the maximum benefit of all members. Each member contributes according to their capabilities. The needs of less capable members are augmented by more capable members. Communism is one version of socialism that has worked in some societies and continues today. Unfortunately, there are many cases where the socialistic form of government has failed to reach the idealistic goal and failure has caused great hardship. Regardless of how the central government was formed, it frequently used its power excessively and leaders emerge that became dictators. Members lost their feeling of responsibility, anomie increased, and productivity declined.

The opposite structure is democracy where the government is controlled directly by the members. When this is done by a direct vote of the members, it is the majority that rules, creating an excess influence of a self-centered uninformed populace. Various ways have been used to reduce this problem such as voting for selected representatives that are more informed or restricting voting to those that can read and write. Federalism as implemented in the United States reduces the populist power by increasing power of constituent states. Democracies have not always had continuing success because as the members vote themselves more benefits, the government becomes unable to meet demands.

In between the extremes of socialism and democracy are many other forms of government which likewise have had limited success. The "mandate of heaven" gave many rulers not just political but also religious powers. Here too, though, rulers frequently exceeded their mandate and dictatorial actions created such hardships that revolt terminated the mandate. Even the benevolent despotisms of the Enlightenment age did not last despite their idealistic beginning. Analysis of the many forms of government is not in the scope of this article. The purpose here is to show the importance of recognizing the perennial conflict between individual and communal interests and the need for people to consider this issue. That would raise levels of consciousness and stimulate the development not only for better government, but also for greater advancement of human nature. Thinking along these lines would provide more meaning and sense of purpose than thinking dominated by "getting and spending."

So why has no social structure emerged that meets the needs of its members with continuing success and without conflict and hardship? How can the welfare of "have-nots" be provided without reducing their creativity and productivity? And how can the "haves" be prevented from imposing political power and conflict? No system yet implemented succeeds. Even the well-thought-out system of checks and balances in the United States has problems.

The answer takes us back to human nature. No form of government will succeed until a massive change in thinking occurs. A consciousness must emerge that includes awareness of this situation with concern about a long-range solution that subjugates personal gratification to the good of humanity. This would make personal existence more manageable, continuation more secure, and greater feeling-good flourishing. Media, educators, and leaders should emphasize this need rather than the consumerism, violence, and aggression currently emphasized. If more people would "think on these things," consciousness would emerge faster to consolidate the goals of individuals, communities, and civilization.

It seems to me that God designed us to live in society—Just as He has given the bees honey;
And as our social system could not exist
Without the sense of justice and injustice,
He has given us the power to acquire that sense.
(Voltaire, Discours sur l'Homme, 1776)

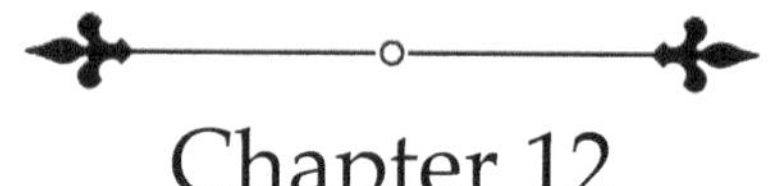

Chapter 12

Meaningful: Mil from PIL

Are the things you do meaningful? They are if you feel good about them. You climb out of bed in the morning, trundle off to work, struggle to meet goals, and hopefully find time in the evening to relax in front of the TV. You may think the purpose is only to have a paycheck coming in each month, but to be meaningful, a lot more is involved. The underlying reason you do these things is to feel good about your life as well as your daily activities. It is not just because you are here and need the money, it is because you have within you an innate need not only for meaning in daily activities, but also for meaning beyond that of your daily mundane activities for existence, to the meaning of that existence its-self. This is called "meaning-in-life" (MIL).

The innate need to reach out for meaning of life involves something bigger and better than personal day to day activities. It can easily be subdued by the more pressing immediate daily needs; in which case it may ferment in suppressed recesses of the mind where it can cause feelings of dissatisfaction or bubble up to cause feelings of depression and anxiety. However, it has been such a conscious concern in history that it has stimulated the advance of civilization. It is the foundation for religions that in various forms has dominated societies throughout known history. Religious beliefs tend to fill this need for meaning, and they affect non-believers also because of their cultural influence.

Meaningful is generally defined as having meaning or purpose and is associated with both short-range immediate goals and long-range idealistic goals. Even though going to work each morning is not reaching out for something bigger and better beyond daily activity, it is meaningful because it provides a "sense of purpose." This has been generalized into the term "purpose-in-life" (PIL).

It was the Austrian psychiatrist Viktor Frankl (1997) that popularized PIL as a result of his experiences in Nazi prison camps during World War II. He noted that those prisoners that had a goal beyond daily existence were more able to endure the rigors of captivity and to survive. After the war, he related this to his medical practice and became famous for his statement about the difficulty of over one-third of his patients as being caused by lacking a goal that gave them a sense of purpose for their life. To treat this, he developed Logotherapy that has been effective particularly for depression, anxiety, and alcoholism.

For Dr. Frankl, it does not make much difference what the person's goal is as long as that person has one. Research at St Louis University demonstrated that the nature of that goal is also important and is related to the person's health, well-being, and performance (Wheeler, 2019). The most effective goals were aimed at something outside of the self, that provided a sense of contribution, and involved a search for understanding. This has been supported by other research started by psychologist Martin Seligman (2011) and medical researcher George Vaillant (2008), and related to MIL by psychologist Roy Baumeister (2005).

There is now reputable support beyond belief and assumption that for greatest well-being a person's daily activities should be based on purposes related to a long-range sense of an externally oriented PIL. That, in turn, provides a satisfying sense of MIL (Wheeler, 2019). How much better our society would be if our media, politicians, and educators emphasized these things, and less about wealth, power, and aggression. People would be more aware of their most basic innate need, their basic motivation that was explained in Chapter 2. Life would be more meaningful and daily activities would be more enjoyable.

Chapter 13

Nature, God, & Consciousness

The terms nature, God, and consciousness represent major ways of explaining the source and meaning of our existence, and each is widely subscribed to and generally considered to represent useful explanations of existence. For nature, existence is the result of evolved physical matter through materialism. For God, a supreme deity designed, started, and may now influence our existence through theism. And for consciousness, some form of mentality through idealism is the prime constituent of existence. Are each of these different views of reality valid? And is it important?

Taking importance first involves recognizing that all of us have a need to provide for meaning and source of existence, and particularly for the reason of one's own life. This could be called philosophy of life, worldview, or ontological imperative explained in Chapter 2. For many, it is pushed into recesses of the subconscious mind by more pressing needs of daily tasks, surfacing as a nebulous feeling of dissatisfaction, depression, or anxiety. But for many others it is a conscious concern (Wheeler, 2019). History and sociology show that it was a driving force behind religions that have dominated societies. Psychology and anthropology show that religious type organizations developed to meet this and other needs such as interpersonal relations, belongingness, social support, authority, object of worship, and salvation. So, whether your ontological imperative is met by materialism, theism, or idealism, or regardless of conscious concern, it is important for health, well-being, and performance. Many of our problems would be alleviated if our media, leaders, politicians, and educators would emphasize these needs rather than needs for power, violence, wealth, and thrill.

Do these three approaches conflict, are they complimentary reflecting different domains of explanation, or could each be valid as emerging from something more fundamental? The answer to all is yes, depending on the level of consideration. The proposal here is that at the most fundamental level we can handle, there seems to be a common fundamental constituent (FC). This is most clear in the materialism approach supported by theoretical physics and various branches of sub-atomic science that have objectively supported constituents such as strings, vibrations, fields, forces, and energy that in turn have an FC still being sought. This ultimate FC has been supported by indirect observation and theorized to be something like information, consciousness, intelligence, zero-point energy, hyperdimension, etc. (Kuhlmann, 2013). The nature of this type of FC is appreciated in the materialistic approach because matter is recognized as mainly fuzzy space containing forces that create the hard surfaces we feel as physical material. The particles that have been detected in atoms are separated by these forces and seem to consist of nebulous things that could also be based on an ultimate FC. Recently proposed theories of Multiverse and Many Worlds even support alternate realities where unknown worlds could exist with different forms of matter and different FCs (Haisch, 2010; Wheeler, 2019).

The approach of theism proposes an FC that is easiest to grasp, best defined, and most popular: however, it results from subjective experience and has the least scientific support. Because we live in a "cause & effect" environment and have such a strong need for a "first cause," various forms of a supernatural deity have developed such as God, Allah, and Brahman. Belief in such deity effectively provides for a graspable FC and cause of existence.

In between these two approaches is idealism supported by recent studies of a consciousness that exists as a universal "cosmic force," an FC from which the material world developed. Personal consciousness of an individual is proposed as an aspect of that FC. The consciousness approach has support from quantum physics as being related to some form of intelligence or mental activity that caused potentialities to coalesce (Polkinghorne, 2007). It is supported in psychology as a type of mental force called psi or collective consciousness (Radin, 2013). This relates to the "hard problem" of how immaterial consciousness can arise from physical brain activity; however, it seems reasonable that a form or aspect of an idealistic FC could carry over to personal human awareness (Rue, 2006). There is even support from information technology for a human's personal consciousness to be related to a primal universal consciousness and thus be an aspect of such an FC (Lohrey 2018).

Each of the three approaches emerged from experiences, observations, and need for explanation. Each has a way of explaining many mysterious phenomena that have eluded science. Each developed terms for an FC, but none seem adequate. A term unencumbered by excess meanings is needed. One might be Ontos, the ancient Greek word for fundamental being. Other candidates are: Is, More, It,

Cause, Aether, or maybe even God. Further discussion about FC is in the next chapter.

This is a big jump from our perception of the chair I am sitting on as being solid enough to support my body to viewing the chair as consisting of the nebulous non-physical force. However, if you can believe what scientists say, you can think that it is possible, and you can feel that at the most fundamental level there is some kind of non-material-like constituent yet to be uncovered.

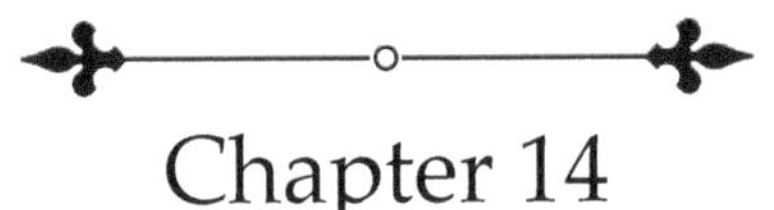

Chapter 14

Science and Cognition

We all want our daily activities and our life in general to be comfortable, manageable, and meaningful. To have this we need to feel that we can influence important things, that things have some predictability and explanation, and that the chair I am sitting on will not revert to a nebulous field of mystical force. We live in a cause-and-effect environment, and we have an innate need for an explanation that provides cause for our experiences. Science is the study of things that can be objectively observed and is concerned with reliable explanations, but it can only deal with observables excluding deep explanations of ultimate concerns and causes beyond observables of material nature. On the other hand, cognition is thinking about things independent of observation. It is the subjective mental process that produces insight, revelation, speculation, and belief that can fill in and provide explanations beyond science, however as human deductions they are subject to error and sometimes conflict with scientific findings. As used here, cognition is a basis of religious and supernatural explanations. Despite conflicts, both science and cognition seem to be needed—science that enables explanation and use of our observable environment, and cognition that enables explanation and use of the mysterious environment inaccessible to science. The latter frequently invokes supernatural explanations that conflict with the natural explanations of science. Do we need both natural and supernatural explanations?

At one time the explanation of causes was quite limited. Our primitive ancestors knew that sunshine caused their body to get warm and that the sun could be considered the cause. But what caused the sun to be there in the first place? The warmth had a natural explainable cause; however, the sun's presence was a mystery. Explaining the sun's existence required a more basic cause that could only come from cognitive processes involving something beyond nature, something supernatural. Either because of discomfort from that mystery or because of some insight, a supernatural explanation was adopted. This use of a supernatural explanation that alleviated the mystery is now called "God-of-the-gaps." Thus, began religion and belief in supernatural causes. As objective knowledge revealed the sunrise to be a natural terrestrial event, the belief of a supernatural force pushing up the sun was abandoned, and the God-of-the-gaps explanation was questioned. This conundrum exists today. Scientific findings caused natural explanations to replace many supernatural explanations and brought into question the validity of human cognitions that formed religious beliefs and dogma.

Today, natural explanations are available for most phenomena, that is until we marvel about the intricacies of life (such as childbirth and death) or wonder about what is out there beyond our own vision or that of science. Although theories exist, objective information (science) cannot explain why the universe exists or why we are here and where we came from, but supernatural explanations are available. Faith in a supernatural agent has many benefits, not only explanation for our ultimate concerns, but also connections with other people of similar faith. This is the basis for religions with their social organizations that provide material and spiritual support, belongingness, forgiveness, emotional uplift, immortality, and positive regard.

There is a hazy line between naturalism and supernaturalism. Naturalism is defined as the doctrine that physical laws as learned from objective observation are adequate to eventually account for all phenomena. Supernaturalism holds that to account for all phenomena, a transcendent reality beyond our known physical laws is required. Since that reality cannot be observed, it is revealed through human cognition. There are many other definitions for naturalism, supernaturalism, natural, and supernatural, however the ones used here are useful in dealing with the validity of answers to ultimate questions from both scientific information and cognitive revelation.

Science now has the ability to look out in space far enough to observe nebulous phenomena that support theories such as multiverse, many worlds, and multiple dimensions that indicate possibility of alternate realities that are beyond known physical nature and may even involve a supernature. Likewise, science has now been able to look far enough into the atom to see nebulous forces or fields that are beyond known material nature and border on the supernatural. Human cognition is now using findings from sub-atomic physics to support the fundamental constituent of matter as being something similar to consciousness, information, or intelligence (Kuhlmann, 2013). Is this natural or supernatural? It gets close to things such as spirit, deity, and holy ghost. Some knowledgeable people say that if such constituents exist, they would be part of nature or an alternate aspect of nature.

On the other hand, some knowledgeable people say that these new findings can only be explained as a reality not bounded by our known laws of physics, or as an alternate supernatural reality that may even contain deity. So, the line between naturalism and supernaturalism is obscure and both may be needed to answer ultimate questions about existence. Anything is possible, but we have to live in the world as it presents itself to us here and now. Reliable natural explanations are now available for most daily experience providing sensible proximate local causes, and for distal ultimate causes, reliable support for supernatural explanations is also now available. Despite the uncertainty of unlimited possibilities, recognizing probability of supernatural explanations helps us handle mysterious events. We need naturalism to explain proximate local cause and we need supernaturalism to explain distal ultimate cause. Supernaturalism could include phenomena whose cause is natural but not yet known as well as phenomena whose cause might be a different reality transcendent to known laws of physics, and objective study of supernaturalism is worthy of consideration.

Closely related to the natural-supernatural issue is the physical-metaphysical issue. Physics is a branch of science that deals with matter and energy and their interaction. As a science it is limited to observables and phenomena free of personal opinion or belief. Metaphysics is a branch of philosophy that deals with the fundamental nature of reality and being beyond the reaches of physics. It literally means beyond or after physics so it can include opinion and belief; however, as a branch of philosophy it has traditionally attempted to use physics information with logic and bottom-up reasoning. Religion has always been a part of philosophy despite a top-down approach, and many religions and their study (theology) refer to their metaphysical nature. Of interest here is the advance of physics into the fundamental nature of matter where bottom-up explanations merge with top-down explanations of metaphysics

When I was in high school chemistry, in the front of the classroom on the wall behind the teacher's desk was the Periodic Chart of Elements. I do not remember any of the teacher's lectures, but I do remember the picture of that chart. I was impressed with the pattern and structural relationship of the elements. There were 92 elements, basic constituents of our physical world, made up of various combinations of electrons, protons, and neutrons. How elegant! What could account for this pattern and regularity?

That was in 1945. Since then, the chart has been expanded to 112 elements, each of which is made up of not three, but 18 different particles called fermions and 5 forces called bosons (Powell, 2018). The particles have all been found to be made up of 6 types of quarks and leptons. As capabilities of nuclear science increased, constituents of quarks and leptons have been discovered that seem to be nebulous things similar to fields, vibrations, or maybe bundles of properties (Kuhlmann, 2013). Fields are best explained as some form of energy, and scientists are now searching for the nature of this basic form of energy. Quantum theory supports exotic terms such as sygons (Hardy, 2016), psychons (DeBiase, 2009), and noetic fields (Amoroso & Martin, 2002). Such descriptions of energy fields are similar to metaphysical terms used in religions such as spirit, angel, and ghost. Theoretical physicists have recently used preon is a general term that implies a common constituent, the leading candidate for which is a vibrating string (Lincoln,

2012). But what is vibrating? Before "string theory" was organized, the emanant physicist John Wheeler (1997) proposed it was information and there is now a sizable following supporting "information theory." The nature of this information is rather fuzzy and can be related to religion's use of "word" and "light." "In the beginning was the Word and the Word was God" (John 1:1). "And God said, let there be light: and there was light" (Genesis 1:3).

Another popular term now used to describe the fundamental constituent of matter is consciousness. Traditionally consciousness has been considered a product of the human brain, a mental awareness of the environment including awareness of oneself and one's own cognitive process. Much is known about what consciousness does, its levels and states, but attempts to explain how it occurs and how it produces mysterious results have resulted in broadened use of the term. One explanation sees a person's consciousness as an aspect of a universal or cosmic consciousness with which it can interact (Goff, 2019). Quantum mechanics and quantum theory have provided scientific support for consciousness as affecting sub-atomic activity providing a cause referred to as "quantum mind" (Walker, 2000). This aspect of consciousness could explain mysterious functions such as telepathy, psychokinesis, and insight (Radin, 2013). Thus, consciousness representing some form of mental force could be a basic constituent of fermions. This concept is not really new. One of the oldest concepts in metaphysical philosophy is idealism which holds that everything is a result of mental activity (Robinson, 2020) (see Chapter 13). It has been incorporated into most religions as Spirit, Holy Ghost, Atman, God, Brahman, Allah, etc.

It is interesting that the terms being used in physics to explain ultimate constituents of matter are now overlapping with terms that have been used in metaphysics to explain religious beliefs. Is a melding taking place between these fields to explain the make-up of matter? As supernaturalism is needed to answer questions inaccessible to naturalism, metaphysics seems needed to answer questions inaccessible to physics. The divide between science and cognition is decreasing.

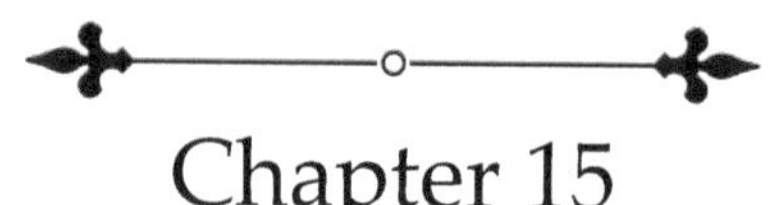

Chapter 15

The Survival of Life

It is widely accepted that the basic goal of life is survival. This means sustenance and reproduction. Even though societies have been concerned throughout known history with belief in some form of salvation or transcendence beyond physical survival, physical existence has been a dominant concern. Physical existence will become even more of concern because science predicts that in about 4 billion years physical existence on Earth will be burned to a crisp, and human life will probably cease in about 1 billion years because of the ultimate global warming. This is when the sun will have expanded and created the ultimate climate change (Shah, 2021; Helmenstine, 2021). Most religions also predict a cessation of current human life or change that produces some form of altered existence although dates are not specified. In theology this is known as eschatology. What will have happened at that time to human life? Does that mean that life as we know it will not survive? New information coming from theoretical physics, cosmology, psychology, and philosophy is producing new ideas about life, particularly human life, that clouds previous predictions. Is science finding that life may be more than physical existence that will burn to a crisp? Could a form of life emerge that survives this destruction of physical matter or maybe becomes a new creation as proposed in many religions, especially Christianity (Hausoul, 2019)?

Quantum mechanics that explains nicely observations of sub-atomic particles has opened science to considerations previously reserved for philosophy and religion. The particles observed in our physical environment have been found to consist of forces and sub-particles that in turn consist of energy forms and fields of nebulous nature. It seems that to explain some recent observations something even more basic than this is needed, something such as intelligence, information, or consciousness (Wheeler, 1997). This implies that our physical world at its most basic level may be non-physical and consequently not subject to physical destruction. When the sun destroys all physical material on earth, could something remain that possibly would build new particles in a different environment (maybe a new creation)? Could human life evolve to a different form that would survive in a different reality?

Recent studies of complexity provide a possible avenue for this scenario. A pattern that jumps out from history and paleontology is the repeated emergence of more complex levels of components in the universe. This could be the result of creative design or it could result from natural evolution. In any case, shortly after the Big Bang sub-atomic particles melded in a mysterious way to form atoms with increased complexity and new emergent characteristics that were more than the "sum of its parts" (McCall, 2010).

Next on the scale of complexity are molecules which are combinations of atoms that once again melded in a mysterious way and likewise interacted to form more complex chemical compounds. As molecules interacted with each other another mysterious thing developed, life.

Molecules in combination learned to reproduce and melded into complex organizations that facilitated existence and reproduction. This is studied by the field of biology that now admits that the mysterious way that life starts, and proceeds is influenced by unknown factors, and that the emergence of life cannot be explained by looking only at its basic parts (Service, 2015).

Life systems of molecules combined to form vegetation, animals, and ultimately humans with ever increasing complexity. The field of biology gives way to the various fields of human physiology and psychology that are making strides in explaining the fascinating ways in which the human body grows, reproduces, and declines. A special feature of human life is the brain which is more complex than any other known thing. The new field of neuroscience combines many classic fields to study how the brain operates, how it produces the mind with sophisticated capabilities of information processing that vastly improved survivability; and how the mind produces consciousness, an awareness of mind processes that produces concerns about the process itself, why it exists, what its purpose is, and its future (Jeeves & Brown, 2009). Personal consciousness has been found to interact with both internal body processes and external factors such as other people, things, and external sources of information. Fascinating new findings are continually being announced, but as more is known deeper mysteries involving unknown factors and possibilities develop.

The next level of complexity developed as humans realized their dependence on each other. Like molecules, they self-organized into groups that facilitated existence and reproduction. Collective minds with astounding abilities emerged from socialized individuals, and it was realized that there is a pattern to the increasing complexity of human existence. The fields of anthropology, sociology, and history have demonstrated a continuing human development that advanced civilization and culture in both efficiency and complexity (Baumeister, 2005).

It took millions of years for living organisms to emerge with a brain capable of processing information, and then many more years to emerge with the use of conscious awareness that we have today. Science indicates that about 1 billion years are available for further development of human life and if past increases in complexity continue, untold forms of life may emerge in that time. It is even possible that as solar heat builds up, human adaptability may overcome characteristics subject to material destruction of nature and continue in a post-solar system. If the basic constituent of matter is non-material (consciousness, information, intelligence, super-mind, etc.), could a form of life emerge that is not affected by the destruction of matter? It is a long shot, but already human efforts are showing potential. Developments about artificial intelligence are indicating feasibility of a computerized entity that far exceeds current human mental ability. The transhuman movement is using medical advances in gene editing and body modification aimed at producing a "superhuman" (Tirosh-Samuelson, 2012). And the Psychotronic Association is bridging research about science, spirit, mind, and technology to explore human potential. Such efforts could produce a new emergent form of life surpassing current limitations. There are physical and moral dangers in these efforts of "tinkering with life" and "playing God," but even theologians are supporting similar efforts (Weissenbacher, 2018).

The famous French Jesuit priest, geologist, and paleontologist Teilhard de Chardin (1965) supported spiritual evolution as the purpose of existence and a plan of God. It will continue until humans reach the "omega point." He is not clear about appropriateness of human interventions into the natural process, nor is he clear if this can occur before material life is destroyed. A recent issue of the Journal *Theology and science (16(3), 2018)* was devoted to articles about human progress toward a transcendent state known as deification, sanctification, or divination in religion with the question of appropriateness of human intervention.

Many of the writers indicated this was God's intention. Irenaeus, a famous Greek philosopher, established an early Christian position in the second century CE when he advocated that God created the universe so that a living organism would evolve naturally by overcoming the problems of material existence and meeting the challenges of evil with their own ingenuity. The respected English physicist and theologian, John Polkinghorne (2007), proposed that our Creator's purpose was two stepped. First was the current creation existing at some distance from a veiled Creator so that creatures will have the freedom to make themselves, and then the second step is the creatures encounter with the unveiled riches of the divine creator's nature. He goes further to say that it is possible that God could create a form of matter not subject to the decay characterizing material of this world. Most religions provide for a non-material realm where personal consciousness continues after bodily death and can exist in places such as heaven, nirvana, and jannah.

Another approach in theology is the view of God is a universal type of consciousness of which individual human consciousnesses are aspects. Both develop together as proposed by Panentheism and Process Theology (Simpson, 2013). The "omega point" proposed by Teilhard de Chardin (1965) is the time when we have developed a personal consciousness that melds with the universal consciousness. Eastern religions also support this approach with concepts such as reincarnation, Atman, and Brahman. Humans as a species have only about a billion years to complete their transition. The human organism has evolved tremendous abilities during its known history of about 2.5 million years and if nuclear war or some other mishap does not occur in the next billion years, it could fulfill religious predictions and be compatible with science.

More important than these intentional efforts of either human or God for the survival of life, is a natural trend that seems to be occurring. Several surveys and statistical analyses reported by organizations such as Gallop Poll, Pew Research Center, and Public Religion Research Institute are showing a major drop for belief in traditional religions and attendance in religious activities (PewForum, 2019). However, participation in non-traditional religious activities is increasing as are concerns about spirituality and God. This has been happening in Europe for many years and is now pronounced in the United States. The major cause of this shift has been associated with the recent publicity about research findings and personal experiences that raise questions about explanations and dogma provided by traditional religions. Major changes are occurring in religious beliefs to make them more sensible, and these changes are modifying culture and influencing lifestyle changes.

It is well established that the complexity of human thinking has developed over time. The earliest known forms of belief attributed animal and human characteristic to supernatural forces resulting in superstitious forms of animism and shamanism that became more sophisticated with time. In addition to explaining cause of mysterious phenomena, these systems met many other needs such as ordering community activities, establishing acceptable behavior, and providing physical and mental support. Most importantly they provided a culture of conduct, ethics, and morals that were exemplified in behavior, the things people did. Not all people were believers, however even the non-believers were subjected to the prevailing culture that established acceptable behavior and direction for actions in their society.

Around the period from 700BCE to 200BCE major changes occurred in cognitive ability and belief systems that laid the foundations for the major religions of today. Laozi started Taoism emphasizing a harmonious naturalness; Confucius laid the foundation for social humanism; Buddha gave people power to influence their future; Zoroaster introduced original goodness that must be reclaimed; and Judaism was revitalized with miraculous events. Christianity and Islam grew out of these movements. This period has been termed the "axial age" and seemed to result from the development of sophisticated abilities to consider new situations and events without primitive superstitions (Armstrong, 2000).

By the eighteenth-century CE, these religions had become so well established that cultures of dogma, faith, worship had difficulty adjusting to growing knowledge setting the stage for another major change in belief systems and culture. The Enlightenment was an age of revolt against authoritarian political and religious powers that conflicted with the advance of knowledge and objective thinking. The world had emerged from the "dark ages" and was adjusting to new-found freedom, knowledge, and prosperity. The major religions that survived adjusted also (Armstrong, 2000).

Today, once again major changes are occurring that shake the foundation of belief systems with their religious housing and impact on culture. People world-wide are recognizing for the first time that war and military force could destroy the world but continue to be necessary to solve global conflict and stop tyranny; that negotiation and cooperation are failing; that self -interests of political powers and economic networks are sacrificing individual well-being and widening the gap between rich and poor; that failure of schools to provide useful education is increasing; and finally that nature's ability to support human increase in longevity is over taxed because of demands and abuses of increased population. Traditional sources of meaning, purpose, and guidance are being questioned and modified as occurred during the axial age and the Enlightenment. We may be in the advent of a second axial age or a second Enlightenment—a period of major changes in the institutionalized belief systems that have dominated societies and organized culture. These major changes occurring in thinking, meaning, purpose, culture, and consciousness have many current indications.

One indication of major change is a universal feeling of crisis. Fear of climate-change is now world-wide. Also, around the world, governmental powers are being over-thrown leading to drastic turmoil and hardship. Particularly in the Middle East and Africa. The upsetting of dominating political powers has released sectarian and tribal violence shocking the world. In the United States, dissatisfaction with the efficiency and cost of government services is calling for drastic changes. Traditional culture is undergoing change because of issues such as inequality, injustice, and racism. People are realizing that human existence is vulnerable, and that if changes in direction are not made, the exhaustion of our environment's ability to support our existence will be hastened.

Another strong indication is the change in religious demographics. Recent polls in the United States indicate that about 90% of the population believe in some form of supernatural deity that started the universe and may continue to exert influence; however, participation in traditional religious activities has dropped precipitously (PewForum, 2019). In between the fundamentalist believers and the atheistic deniers is a growing group known as "nones." These are people accepting a religious culture but denying association with beliefs of the traditional religions. Included are those saying they are spiritual but not religious. Spirituality is a popular term for an attitude of concern about a transcendent force signifying a meaning and purpose higher or better than those of merely meeting immediate needs (see Chapter 4). This is a recognition that there might be some transcendent power, but dissatisfaction with dogmatic views of traditional religions. Related to this is a resurgent interest in "big questions" concerning why we are here, how things got started, and where are we going (Wheeler, 2019). Now that we know so much about what is going on, we can use our knowledge in an attempt to make life more satisfying and the world more comfortable if we can transcend dominance of self-gratification, competition, and empowerment.

Direction for change is emerging from many sources. Growing in popularity is use of the term "flourishing" resulting from research in psychology, philosophy, neuroscience, and interdisciplinary studies of history, sociology, anthropology, and medicine. This movement is supporting a philosophy of life that tolerates differences of opinion and social custom, and provides a purpose of striving for "eudaimonia," a feeling of satisfaction that one is thriving and that one's actions are contributing to the well-being of oneself and of society (Flanagan, 2009). This is more than just being happy (see Chapter 10). It means having a feeling of meaning for one's own life in the face of adversities and seemingly meaningless situations. It recognizes that there is much beyond our current knowledge, that anything is possible, but that we must live in the world as it presents itself to us and manage affairs to the best of our ability. It preserves respect for the mysteries of existence without requiring non-logical explanations.

There are also other movements developing but flourishing seems to have most potential for breaking enough people away from self-centered striving for material wealth and physical comforts to cause society to break away from self-interested power struggles that become ends in themselves. Actions of individuals, politicians, organizations, and businesses could be reoriented to reflect a culture based on human well-being and creative development rather than profit, comfort, and entertainment. Culture and religion can revitalize, and global conflicts can be replaced with cooperation and joint effort.

Adjusting traditional religious beliefs to be compatible with newfound knowledge and tolerance may shake some faith, but by making beliefs more logical and less conflicting, the benefits of religion would be more available to both believers and non-believers. This means accepting a pluralism of reality that includes possibilities of other realities including transcendent divine power, while living in the world as it presents itself to us here and now. Such a foundation for religious faith could be called "pragmatic pluralism," (Chapter 7) and has the potential for empowering people of faith, for enlightening the increasing number of unaffiliated spiritual seekers, and for encouraging those wanting a sense of meaning that comes from having a higher purpose in life.

Such a rejuvenation of culture and religion has the potential to restore the vitality, creativity, productiveness, and power that constitute the "American way of life," and produce an effective defense against threatening aggression. The gospel message will be not only inspiring and beneficent; it will also be helpful, knowledgeable, and sensible.

This is a great vision of the future. Civilization has steadily developed, and it will continue; however, it must be recognized that at the present time not all societies are in the same stage. There are still some societies and nations that use or support aggressive violence to pursue intolerant goals. In these situations, only physical power is respected. Consequently, pacification, negotiation, and beneficence may need to lag behind use of military force. The United States, particularly, must carefully consider the appropriateness of inactivity, diplomacy, and military force. If a threat occurs and diplomacy is ineffective, military force should be used without hesitation, keeping in view the long-range goals of tolerance, respect, responsibility, and pragmatic pluralism.

Despite advances, there are clouds on the horizon. The nuclear age has brought massive capabilities that could destroy human life prematurely. Exploitation of natural resources and population increase could trigger a breakdown in sustainability snuffing out human life before we are ready. Can a form of life emerge that surmounts these ominous probabilities? Could a form of life emerge that can survive the destruction of physical matter as we know it?

As we move from explanations of existence based on particles and forces to explanations based on information, consciousness, and intelligence, life becomes less vulnerable to future destruction. There are probably 1 billion years available for further changes to take place in human nature and for new forms of life to emerge. To achieve this, though, major changes in human nature must occur. The shifting base for values and faith are causing social upheavals, and acceptance of any major changes will be difficult. People must become oriented toward contributing to civilization's advancement; toward improving existence for all rather than focusing only on one's personal gratifications. Would it not be nice if governments, media, education, businesses, and religions were supporting this task instead of their current emphasis on political, economic, and ideological aggression and domination? The replacement of aggression, conflict, and extremism with cooperation, tolerance, and peace would not only reduce violent competition but would also make daily life more meaningful and manageable, and it would alleviate a major source of stress, anxiety, and depression. Furthermore, it may prevent human-made catastrophe and facilitate emergence of a form of life resistant to that ultimate global warming. Can we use the next billion years to continue development of a human consciousness that will survive destruction of physical matter? Chapter 16 has an answer.

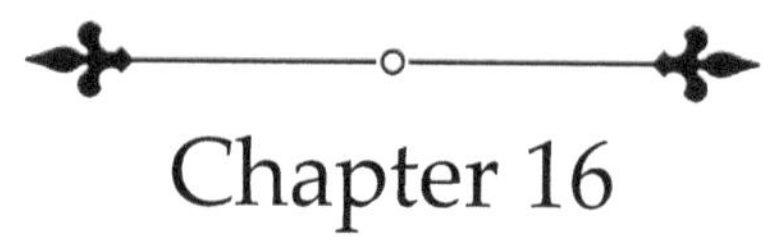

Chapter 16

Moving Forward

It may not be obvious and may even seem far-fetched, but there is more to life than struggling out of bed in the morning, going to work, wrestling with problems all day, and maybe relaxing in front of the TV in the evening. Sure, the first and most pressing purpose in life is to live. Reproduction comes next followed by security for continuation in meeting these pressing needs. But there is more.

Studies of history and paleontology show a continual development in nature toward increasing complexity that enables more effective ways of existing. We modern day humans are the result of this process. There is a pattern of emergent capabilities that seems to have purpose and design. Whether this was the result of a supernatural Great Creator, or the result of a mysterious evolutionary increase in complexity, is not as important as realizing that this advance of nature exists. Primordial forces combined to form atoms which combined to form molecules which, in turn, combined to form living cells which combined to form animals from which developed humans. Humans with their mental abilities combined to form societies and civilization. A purposeful pattern of increasing complexity is indicated. So, here we are, people with sophisticated mental abilities that realize we are part of a developing pattern that has a purpose to increase in complexity—a continuing process rather than a short-range goal.

The most logical result from looking at this view of history is that our fundamental purpose is to continue this pattern of development. This seems to be the purpose in life that spawns many goals. A first goal is to increase our effectiveness so that the daily activities of existence are easier and more comfortable. This requires additional skill, resources, and knowledge. A second goal is to have relations with and support from others. There is no animal more dependent on the fellow member of its species than the human. Family, tribe, community, state, and nation are structured to meet this need resulting in many complications such as individual vs community, altruism vs self-interest, cooperation vs competition, aggression, and war.

A third goal grows out of the first two. We have a mental structure that requires sufficient explanation of our existence that our activities are manageable, and meaningful. This has been referred to as worldview, philosophy of life, religious belief, etc. It results from the same mental structure that causes realization of the need to grow in complexity and development, to wonder about the cause of all of this, why I am here, where I came from, and where I am going. These are known in psychology as ultimate concerns (Emmons, 1999) and result from an ontological imperative (Chapter 2). Despite the amazing advance of science, studies of nature have been unable to provide answers to these concerns, so supernatural explanations developed with spiritual and religious beliefs that have dominated societies throughout known history and have been the main impetus for the advance of science, technology, and civilization.

Religion and culture have traditionally ameliorated ultimate concerns by organizing belief systems that not only give answers and explanation, but also provide resources, support, social structure, and interpersonal relationships. These provisions have made ultimate concerns less pressing, so they have become subjugated to more pressing concerns of daily existence. The ultimate concerns are eclipsed by consumerism, wealth, competition, politics, and aggression, but they are still there. They lie in the recesses of the subconscious mind creating an unsettling feeling of discontent and may boil up to create emotional turmoil resulting in the current increase in depression, anxiety, and suicide. Even the people that do not hold the beliefs of religion and culture live in an environment thusly dominated. Instead of reaching out for a long-range goal of development, most people mainly pursue short-range goals of meeting immediate needs and desires.

The role of a sense of purpose, feeling of meaning in life, and provision for ultimate concerns are widely recognized as being important for mental health and social issues. Many remedial programs and therapies have been developed for individuals, but problems of discontent continue to increase. Many factors have been proposed for causes of these problems such as: decline in religion due to conflicts between dogma and science; cultural emphasis on consumerism, wealth, and competition; loss of family and community ties; increase in mobility; availability of entertainment and other self-centered activities; and delegation of caregiving and responsibility to government. However, these are all ramifications of the more basic cause of losing sight of the growth purpose and its need to provide for explanation.

If this innate need for development and answers to ultimate concerns are so important, why are they so neglected? The answer is because we are lazy. We take the easy path. We adopt procedures and explanations that are expeditious for meeting immediate needs. As commercialization developed, providing for these immediate needs became paramount and formed direction for society. Efforts to explain ultimate concerns were replaced with efforts to meet immediate needs. Progressive Western culture became dominated with "getting and spending," buying and selling material needs. Competition for resources produced conflict, aggression, and violence. Today our major concerns are meeting these material needs. We are bombarded with these goals by TV, radio, newspapers, and magazines. Schools and colleges teach predominantly about these goals with little about ultimate concerns. Leaders and politicians are concerned mainly with their own power and success rather than with ultimate concerns.

How different our world would be if media, educators, leaders, and politicians would emphasize the basic need we all have to understand, develop, and grow rather than the current emphasis on consumerism, wealth, self-interest, and power. This would reorient a focus on existence to a higher goal of moving forward. It would stimulate a constructive sense of purpose that would reduce discontent, depression, and anxiety for individuals, and for nations it would stimulate cooperation instead of conflict and war.

Many causes have been proposed for the current global and personal problems. And many remedies have also been proposed; however, they all will be ineffective until the emergence of a culture dominated by efforts to move forward toward something bigger and better than our current nature. Emergent well-being and peace are possible, and despite the current neglect, history indicates a trend in that direction is occurring.

It is useful to look at the two major aspects of this trend in order to reduce its neglect and speed it up. One called phylogeny is change that has occurred over eons of years in our human species. The other called ontogeny is the pattern of change that occurs in individual humans over their life span from birth to death. Recapitulation theory which states, "ontogeny recapitulates phylogeny" (Heckel, 1992) became popular in the late nineteenth century and was used by Sigmund Freud in his neurosis work. It is still used to explain aspects of development.

Anthropology is the field of study that has provided most information about human phylogeny. Different researchers have proposed different timelines and stages; however, most agree that our unique line of descent started about seven million years ago when a group of higher primates emerged with a larger brain capacity that enabled them to find food more efficiently. Brain capacity and cognitive ability continued to develop, and three million years ago "homo erectus" emerged with the ability to travel away from its habitat. Its members moved beyond their native environment in Africa meeting new challenges that further increased brain capacity and cognitive ability. By 100,000 years ago they had multiplied forming societies considered the first civilizations in Egypt, Mesopotamia (Iraq), and India. Shortly thereafter they expanded to China and Australia, and about 15,000 years ago reach the Americas. This required a lot of courage and cognitive ability because they did not have autos, ships, or airplanes. Archeologists that do the foot work for anthropologists indicate that religious activity had started by then to support the Christian dogma about humans being created about 10,000 years ago. That was when the sophisticated human thinking ability emerged. As cognitive ability and knowledge increased, language developed and by 5,000 years ago writing and city-states had begun. Another milestone was about 3,000 years ago when religious organizations emerged followed by the start of Christianity 2,000 years ago. (Pfeiffer,1969)

This phylogenetic sequence of change in human development indicates a pattern of increased biological, cognitive, and experiential (knowledge) complexity over the years that has parallels with the ontogenetic sequence of changes in humans over their life span. The human infant comes into this world with a blank experiential slate, but has a preprogrammed inherent need to explore, learn, and understand its environment. It increases in complexity biologically, cognitively, and experientially (learning). Its complexity increases continually interspersed with stages of emergent change. Many theories and schemes have been proposed to explain and make sense of this progression. The attached table outlines some of the more useful theories. They are arranged by their emphasis on stages of development starting on the left with the ages of commonly accepted biological stages. Some of these theories emphasize dimensions rather than stages and are on the right side of the table. In the middle of the table are some that include both. Closely related to biological developments is the psychosexual approach of Sigmund Freud (1965) that emphasizes balance and reduction of stress due mainly to sexual concerns.

Jean Piaget's theory (1954) of cognitive development emphasizes adaption through stages of thinking which are related to brain changes. Erik Erikson's psychosocial theory (1964) emphasizes order and unity by resolution of conflicts typical at various stages of age (this is most applicable to people of Western culture). Another useful psychosocial theory is by Jane Loevinger (1973) emphasizing stages of ego development (also based on Western culture). Laurence Kohlberg (1973) organized a theory based on different stages of moral concerns.

Breaking with the pure stage approach is Abraham Maslow's theory (1968) of expansion by meeting categories of needs. Although the categories are based on biological age, they are not prepotent, that is a person may be concerned about any of the categories at any time, however resolving one stage facilitates meeting needs of the next stage This is expanded in the last column (page 115) by the Wheeler theory (2019) that emphasizes stages of pursuing meaning that can be active at any age as dimensions. The final row at the bottom of the table shows ultimate higher levels (meta-stages) that have been proposed for some of the theories (see Chapter 4).

Notice that most of these theories have a stage or dimension that represents a high level of motivation, a level of activity concerned with something bigger and better than everyday activities of existence. This gives the feeling of moving forward individually and contributing to the advance of humanity. People can experience this good feeling of moving forward at any age if they can reach out for something beyond self-centered daily activity.

This is our destiny and the essence of what it all means. If we can relax and pursue it, individuals will develop a sense of constructive purpose and meaning that will not only reduce crime and violence, but will reduce depression, anxiety, and suicide. Globally it will reduce aggression, terrorism, and war. Most importantly, though, it will facilitate the complex development of the human mind so that life may resist the inevitable human physical demise. At any time, human life as we know it could become extinct, but hopefully we have about a billion years to work on it before the ultimate climate change occurs and the sun's heat destroys human life as we know it. Although progress seems inevitable, it would be enhanced by recognizing the need and pursuing it directly, A by-product of such a reemphasis would be greater well-being and comfort for both individuals and societies.

Developmental Systems of Primary Motivation

Stages >			
	Psychosexual	Cognitive	Psychosocial
Age	Freud	Piaget	Erikson
1	Oral	Sensorimotor	Trust
2	Anal	Preoperation	Autonomy
3			
4	Phallic		
5		Concrete-	Initiative
6	Latent	operational	
7			Industry
8			
9			
12			Identity
	Genital	Formal-	
		operational	
18			Intimacy
20			
30	Young adult		
40	Middle age		Generativity
50			
65	Mature		
		Dialectic *	Integrity *

* Meta-stage for transcendent concern

Developmental Systems of Primary Motivation

		<	Dimensions
Ego	Moral	Needs	Purpose
Loevinger	Kohlberg	Maslow	Wheeler
Physical	Authority	Physical	Homeostasis
Symbionic			
	Reciprocity		
Impulsive			Adjustment
Expedient	Social	Security	
Conforming			
	Law-Order		
			Individuality
Conscientious		Belonging	
	Contract		
			Creativity
		Esteem	
	Ethics		
Autonomous			
		Actualization*	Contribution*
Integrated *	Ontologic *		

* Meta-stage for transcendent level of concern

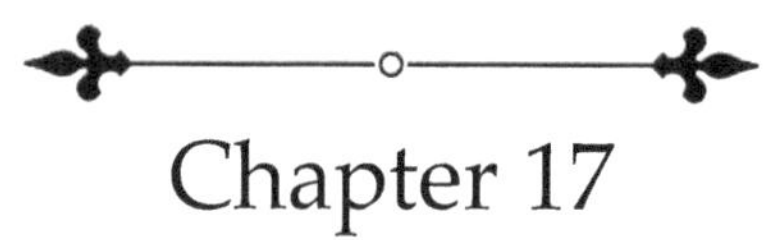

Chapter 17

What, Why and How?

If you have waded through the preceding chapters, you have the right to now ask the questions "what does it all mean, what are we doing, why are we doing it, and how have we and should we be doing it?" The chapters started with the attempt to scientifically support the theory that all thinking humans have within them a need to exist, to continue existence, to find meaning and purpose for that existence, and to search for its explanation. These needs create difficult tasks that involve searching for knowledge about cause of experiences, and it does not stop with cause of immediate daily experiences. It extends to the mysterious unknown of ultimate concerns, why are we here and what is the cause of it all. The answer is allusive and controversial, but whether our existence is the result of design or of evolutionary adaption is not as important as realizing that pursuing the question is in all of us. This we call the ontological imperative. The object of the ontological imperative we call ultimate reality, what started things and what keeps them going. The ontological imperative is buried in all of us as a basic motivation that fuels our daily activities to meet immediate needs. Awareness of this basic motivation stimulates what we call ultimate concerns. The later chapters are about impacts and implications of this basic motivation and about proposed suggestions for how to proceed in its pursuit.

Science has provided overwhelming information about the causes and mechanisms of observed phenomena producing astounding technology and comforts. But science has been unable to explain ultimate reality, origin and cause of our existence. A need for explanation has been so strong in thinking humans that it was filled in with speculation, assumption, insight, and revelation creating beliefs and religions that have dominated societies. Important impacts of beliefs and religion were explored showing their role in the advancement of personal comfort and social civilization, and also showing their shortcomings and adversities. A conclusion was expressed that a major purpose in human life in addition to existence is the pursuit of personal development and contribution to development of the human species. How to do this requires a search for answers to "what and why."

This search into the unknown also raises an issue about the importance of such questions. For many people, the ultimate concerns about ultimate reality are eclipsed by more immediate concerns of daily life. They may be ameliorated by religious or philosophical beliefs, or they are pushed into the recesses of the unconscious mind. In either case, though, they are there and can surface at an inconvenient time or foster a nebulous feeling of dissatisfaction. It is possible that there is no ultimate reality, nothing that started existence or established a purpose and meaning. Indeed, the respected physicist Sean Carroll (2016) stated "There may be no ultimate answer to the "Why?" question. The universe simply is..." (p203). But, even if there is no ultimate reality, having a philosophy of life or worldview that provides for one has been related to better health, well-being, and performance. Whether there is or is not, our destiny seems to include a search for it. Being aware of this need and pursuing it in addition to pursuing immediate daily needs is the "how." If widely pursued, personal problems such as anxiety, depression, and suicide; domestic problems such as criminality and violence; and global problems such as aggression and terrorism would all be reduced. It would stimulate cooperation and mutuality instead of conflict and violence.

So, why are we here? It is to search for meaning and purpose in being here, to help others, and to help humanity's ability for the search. How best can this be done? By being aware of this basic motivation and fostering its pursuit, and by "thinking on these things." How nice it would be if media, politicians, leaders, and educators would emphasize this basic motivation instead of their current emphasis on consumerism, comfort, entertainment, conflict, and power.

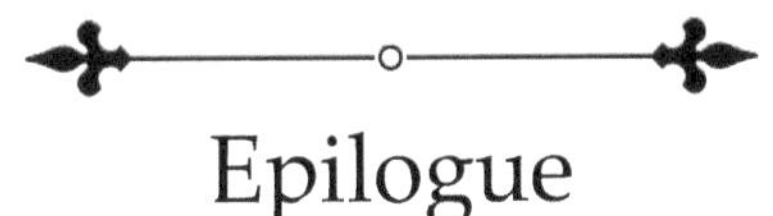

Epilogue

So what? This is all deep stuff about which we seemingly can do little. Is its pursuit beyond us? Is it beyond the capability of our sophisticated scientists, our intellectual philosophers, or our enlightened theologians? The answer is maybe yes; however, hindsight shows advances occurring in the past, and foresight about the future indicates belief in progress is needed for current personal life to be meaningful and manageable. We must flourish in our environment as it is presented to us despite unfathomable possibilities while respecting and pursuing the mysterious unknown. We must meet daily immediate needs and provide for continued development of ourselves, fellow humans, and societies. This requires consideration of questions such as the purpose of it all, is there really an influence beyond current knowledge as believed by many, and if so, what its nature is. The cutting edge right now is the study of consciousness, an awareness of mental activity associated with mind. Is there an aspect of the human mind that can send and receive information beyond the human body by-passing the normal senses, is there a form of life that can survive the ultimate global warming, and is there an aspect of the mind that survives bodily death?

As a research psychologist, I am about to get that last question answered. Earthly demise is something we all will experience, and I agree with Julius Caesar when he said, "it seems to me most strange that men should fear; seeing that death, a necessary end, will come when it will come." The human body is limited in its ability to absorb new knowledge, its ability to adjust to new conditions, and its ability to make contributions. Fresh minds are needed for advances to take place. I am ready to make room for them because I have had more than ninety years to make my contribution. I can now move on to that ultimate question of what happens to consciousness after physical death of the material body—the great experiment in which we all participate.

> "Light breaks where no sun shines;
> Where no sea turtle runs,
> The waters of the heart
> Push in their tides.
> Light breaks where no sun shines
> And death shall have no dominion."
> (Dylan Thomas, 1953)

References

Adler, A. (1979). *Superiority and social interest* (H. Ansbacher and R. Ansbacher Eds.) (3rd Ed.). New York: W.W. Norton.

Allport, G.W. (1955). *Becoming*. New York: Yale University Press.

Amoroso, R. & Martin, B. (2002). *Consciousness: a thousand points of life. Noetic Journal. 3 (4), 289.*

Antonovsky, A. (1987). *Unraveling the mystery of Health: How people manage Stress and stay well*. San Francisco: Jossey-Bass.

Armstrong, K. (2000). *The battle for god*. New York: Knopf.

Aronson, E. (1972). *The social animal*. San Francisco: Freeman.

Attridge, H. (2009). *The religion and science debate*. New Haven: Yale University Press.

Bartlett, J. (1967). *Familiar quotations*. NY: Little, Brown & Co.

Batson, D; Schoenrade, P.; & Ventis, W. (1993). *The religious and the individual: a social-psychological perspective*. New York: Oxford.

Baumeister, R. (2002). Religion and psychology: introduction to the special issue. *Psychological Inquiry, 13(3)*, 165-167.

Baumeister, R. (2005). *The Cultural Animal*. New York: Oxford University Press.

Baxton, D. (2007). Religious naturalism and the future of Christianity. *Zygon, 42(2)*, 317-352. Braisby, N. (1012). *Cognitive psychology*. NY: Oxford University Press USA.

Buhler, C. (1967). Human life goals in the humanistic perspective. *Journal of Humanistic Psychology. 7*, 36.

Calaprice, A. (2005). *The new quotable Einstein*. Princeton, NJ: Princeton University Press.

Campbell, J. (1988). *The power of myth*. New York: Doubleday.

Camus, A. (1960). *The myth of Sisyphus, and other essays*. (J. O'brien, Trans.). New York: Vintage Books.

Carroll, S. (2016). *The big picture*. New York: Dutton.

Chardin, Teillhard (1965*). The phenomenon of man*. New York: Harper & Row.

Clayton, P. & Knapp, S. (2011). *The predicament of belief*. New York: Oxford.

Cloninger, R. (2004). *Feeling good*. New York: Oxford.

Comstock, G. & Partridge, K. (1972). Church attendence and health. *Journal of Chronic Disease, 25 (12)*, 665-672.

Davies, P. (2008). *The goldilocks enigma*. New York: Houghton Mifflin.

Dawkins, R. (2006). *The God delusion*. New York: Houghton Mifflin.

Dennett, D. (2006). *Breaking the spell*. New York: Viking.

DiBiase, F. (2009). A holographic model of consciousness. *Quantum Biosystems. 3*, 207-220.

Einstein, A. (1994). *Ideas and opinions.* NY: Modern Library.

Ellis, G. (2011). Does the universe really exist? *Scientific American*. August, 38-53.

Ellison, C. W. (1983). Toward an integrative measure of health and well-being. *Journal of Psychology and Theology, 19*, 35-48.

Emmons, R. (1999). *The psychology of ultimate concerns*. New York: Guilford.

Erikson, E. (1964). *Insight and Responsibility*. New York: Norton.

Faber, M. (2004). *The psychological roots of religious belief*. Amherst, NY: Prometheus.

Flanagan, O. (2009). *The really hard problem*. Cambridge, MA: MIT Press.

Fowler, J. (1981). *Stages of faith*. San Francisco: Harper.

Frankl, V.E. (1997). *Man's search for ultimate meaning*. New York: Plenum Press.

Freud, A. (1965). Normality and pathology in childhood: Assessments of development. In *Writings (Vol.6*). New York: International Universities Press.

Fromm, E. (1947). *Man for himself*. Greenwich, CT:Fawcett.

Fromm, E. (1973). *The anatomy of human destructiveness*. New York: Holt, Rinehart, & Winston.

Gervais, W., Najle, M., Caluori, N. (2021). The origins of religious disbelief. *Social Psychology and Personality Science.* https://doi.org/10.1177/1948550621994001.

Goff, P. (2019). *Galileo's error: foundations for a new science of consciousness*. NY: Pantheon.

Goodenough, U. (1998). *The sacred depths of nature*. New York: Oxford.

Gould, S. (2006). *The richness of life*. New York: Norton.

Hamer, D. (2004). *The God gene*. New York: Doubleday.

Haisch, B. (2010). *The purpose guided universe*. Franklin Lakes, NJ: Career Press.

Hardy, C. (2016). ISS theory: cosmic consciousness, self, &life beyond death in a hyperdimensional physics. *Journal of Consciousness Exploration & Research. 7 (11)*, 1012-1035.

Harris, S. (2004). *The end of faith: Religion, terror, and the future of religion*. New York: Norton.

Hausoul, R. (2019). Theology and cosmology: call for interdisciplinary enrichment. *Zygon, 54(2)*, 324-336.

Heckel, E. (1992). *The riddle of the universe*. Buffalo, NY: Prometeous.

Heid, M. (2021). Why human beings are hardwired for spirituality and magical thinking. *http://elemental.meduim.com,* 3/12/2021.

Heider, F. (1944). Social perception and phenomenal causality. *Psychological Review, 51*, 358-374.

Helmenstine, A. (2021). 7 extinction level events that could end life as we know it.

ThoughtCo. *http://www.thoughtco.com/extinction-level-events-4158931*, 2/17/2021.

Helminiak, D. (1998). *Religion and the human sciences*. Albany, NY: State University of New York.

Hooker, S. A., Masters, K. S., & Park, C. L. (2017, July 6). A meaningful life is a healthy life. *Review of General Psychology*. Advance online publication. dx.doi.org/10.1037/gpr0000115

Huxley, A. (1944). *The perennial philosophical*. New York: Harper & Row.

James, W. (2006). *A pluralistic universe*. Charleston, SC: Bibliobazaar.

Jeans, J. (1933). *The new background of science*. New York: Macmillion.

Jeeves, M. & Brown, W. (2009). *Neuroscience, Psychology and Religion*. Conshohocken, PA: Templeton Foundation Press.

Jung, C.G. (1938). *Psychology and religion*. London: Yale University Press

Kaufman, G. (2006). *Jesus and creativity*. Minneapolis: Fortress Press.

Kauffman, S. (2008). *Reinventing the sacred*. New York: Basic Books.

Kelly, G. (1955). *The psychology of personal constructs*. New York: Norton.

Kohlberg, L. (1971). The concepts of developmental psychology as the central guide to education. *Proceedings from the conferences on psychology & the process of schooling in the next decade*. Washington, DC: US Office of Education.

Kuhlmann, M. (3013). What is real? *Scientific American*, 41-17.

Kurtz, P. (2007). *What is secular humanism*? Amherst, NY: Prometheus Books. N

Lincoln, D. (2012). The universe is a complex & intricate place. *Scientific American*. 38-43.

Loevinger, J. (1973). Ego development. *Psychoanalysis & Contemporary Science, 2, 77.*

Loftus, E. (1997). Creating false memories. *Scientific American, 277,* 70-75.

Lohrey, A. (2018) *The evolution of consciousness.* Princeton, NJ: ICRL Press.

Kohlberg, L. (1984). *The psychology of moral development.* New York: Addison Wesley

Mackey, A. (1921). *An encyclopedia of Freemasonry.* New York: Masonic History Company.

Maslow, A. (1968). *Toward a psychology of being.* (2nd Ed.). New York: Harper & Row

Maslow, A. (1971). *The farther reaches of human nature.* New York: Viking.

May, R. (1967). *Psychology and the human dilemma.* New York: Norton.

McCall, B. (2010). Kenosis and emergence: a theological synthesis. *Zygon, 45(1),*149-164.

Meyers, D. (2008). *A friendly letter to skeptics and atheists.* San Francisco: Jossey-Bass.

Nelson, J. (2009). *Psychology, religion, and spirituality.* New York: Springer.

Nelson, K. (2011) *The spiritual doorway in the brain.* New York: Dutton.

Newberg, A. (2010). *Principle of neurotheology.* Burlington, VT: Ashgate.

Newberg, A. & D'Aquili, E. (2001). *Why god won't go away.* New York: Ballantine Books.

Paloutzian, R. & Park, C. (Eds.) (2005). *Handbook of the psychology of religion and psychology.* New York: Guilford.

Pihlstrom, S. (2013). *Pragmatic pluralism & the problem of God.* NY: Fordham University Press.

Pert, C. (2006). *Everything you need to know to feel Go(o)d.* Carlesbad, CA: Hay House.

PewForum (2019). *Pew Research Center. www.pewforum.com*, 10/17/2019.

Pfeiffer, J. (1969). *The emergence of man*. New York: Harper & Row.

Pieget, J. (1954). *The construction of reality in the child*. New York: Basic Books

Polkinghorne, J. (2007). Science and religion: Bottom-up style, interface context. *Zygon, 42(3)*, 573-576.

Powell, D. (2018). The standard model. *Discover, JulyAugust*,68-69.

Radin, D. (2013). *Supernormal*. New York: Deepak Chopra Books.

Rican, P. & Janosova, P. (2010). Spirituality as a basic aspect of personality: A cross-cultural verification of Piedmont's model. *International Journal for the Psychology of Religion, 20*, 2.

Robinson, D. (2020). Idealism. *Encyclopedia Britannia*, Britannia. Com.

Rogers, C. (1961). *On becoming a person*. Boston: Houghton Mifflin.

Rotter, J. (1975). Some problems and misconceptions related to the construct of internal versus external control of reinforcement. *Journal of Consulting and Clinical Psychology, 43*, 56-57.

Schwartz, G. (2006). *The G. O. D. experiments*. New York: Atria.

Sedikides, C. (2010). Why does religiosity persist? *Personality and Social Psychology, 14 (1)*, 3-6.

Seligman, M. (2002). *Authentic happiness*. New York: Free Press.

Selligman, M. (2011). *Flourish*. New York: Free Press.

Severin, F. (1973). *Discovering man in psychology*. New York: McGraw-Hill.

Service, R. (2015). Researchers may have solved the end-of-life conundrum. *Science Magazine*, *https://www.sciencemag.org/news/2015/03/*

Shah,K. (2021). Most life on earth will be killed by lack of oxygen in a billion years. *New Scientists, https://www.newscientist.com*, 3/1/2021.

Simpson, Z. (2013). Emergence and non-personal theology. *Zygon, 48(2)*,405-426.

Smith, E. (2017). *The power of meaning*. New York: Crown.

Spilka, B; Hood, R.; Hunsberger, B.; & Gorsuch,R. (2003). *The psychology of religion* (3d Ed.). New York: Guilford.

Stapp, H. (2004). *Mind, matter, and quantum mechanics* (2d Ed). Heidelberg: Springer-Verlag.

Stenger, V. (2003). *Has science found God*? Amherst, NY: Prometheus.

Stephen, C. (2021). Here are 5 fascinating types of universes. *http://www.medium.com,* 3/12/2021

Teilhard de Chardin, P. (1965). *The phenomenon of man*. (B. Wall, Trans.). New York: Harper & Row.

Teo, T. (1009). Editorial. *Journal of Theoretical and Philosophical Psychology, 29 (2)*, 63-64.

Theology and Science (2018). *16(3).*

Tirosh-Samuelson, H. (2012). Transhumanism as a secular faith. *Zygon, 47(4)*,710-734.

Vaillant, G. E. (2008). *Spiritual development*. New York: Broadway Books.

Szocik, K. (2107). *Religion & religious beliefs as evolutionary adaptions*. *Zygon, 52(1)*, 24-51.

Walker, E. (2000). *The physics of consciousness*. Cambridge, MA: Perseus Books.

Wheeler, J. A. (1997). *At home in the universe*. NY: American Institute of Physics.

Wheeler, R.; Munz, D.; & Jain, A. (1990). Life goals and general well-being. *Psychological Reports, 66*, 307-312.

Wheeler, R. (2010). *Mountains and Minds*. Bloomington, IN: Xlibris.

Wheeler, R. (2019). *Climbing higher: answering big questions*. St Louis: OntoScience Press.
Weissenbacher, A. (2018). Moral enhancement and deification through technology. *Theology and Science*, 16(3),243-246.
Wilson, E. O. (2006). *Creation*. NY: Norton.

Author Biography

Robert Wheeler developed a keen interest in the view people have about meaning and purpose in their lives during 20 years of military experience working with people of various cultures as an infantryman, aviator, engineer, advisor, and research & development coordinator. His last assignment before retiring was Chief of the Foreign Technology Office at the U.S. Army Aviation Systems Command. For another 20 years, he filled positions at St Louis University to include Director of Health Promotion Research and adjunct Associate Professor of Psychology. His major work was research about personality characteristics that contribute to health, well-being, and performance. He also developed measuring instruments and performed analyses for health promotion programs from a didactic viewpoint to assist participants, from an evaluation viewpoint to determine effectiveness, and from a research viewpoint to increase knowledge of health enhancement and quality of life improvement. Now retired, his current work is with spirituality as a personality characteristic, and its role in human nature and health. He also remains physically active. In 2014 he set a new Guinness World Book Record as the oldest man to climb Mount Kilimanjaro in Africa.

Index

A

B

C

D

E

F

G

H

I

J

K

L

M

N

O

P

Q

R

S

T

U

V

W

Y

Z

www.ingramcontent.com/pod-product-compliance
Ingram Content Group UK Ltd.
Pitfield, Milton Keynes, MK11 3LW, UK
UKHW040008200726
13854UKWH00001B/97

9 780578 945163